TAKING THE HIGH ROAD

to Social Studies

Book 4

By Arlene Capriola and Rigmor Swensen

Phoenix Learning Resources

St. Louis • New York

ACKNOWLEDGEMENTS

We deeply appreciate the help so willingly given by many people. In particular, we wish to express our debt and gratitude to Josephine Imwalle, Social Studies Coordinator to the Northport (New York)–East North School District, for her guidance and expertise; to Francesca Montague for her tireless efforts in helping us locate information; to William F. Dwyer for technical assistance, and to the teachers and students at Fifth Avenue School for their cheerful and honest feedback.

ISBN: 0-7915-1662-8

1 2 3 4 5 6 7 8 9 0 06 05 04 03 02

TABLE OF CONTENTS

■■

About SQ3R ★★★★★★★★★★★★★★★★★★★★★★★★★★★★★★★

SQ3R is the key to comprehension. The more you know about something before you read it, the better you'll understand it. SQ3R is simple, quick, and efficient.

Study the five steps below..

> You will use SQ3R for every story in this book.

SURVEY

Look through the story quickly.
Read the introductory paragraph.
Then look at all:

> headings and subheadings
> captions
> pictures
> charts
> graphs
> maps
> highlighted or boldface print

QUESTION

Turn them into questions that may be answered in that section. Also read the questions at the end of the story. They give clues to the reading content as well. Also scan all documents as well as the questions in the Constructed-Response section.

HINT: *Look for the answers when you read the article! In this book read the Objective Questions (you don't need to read all the answer choices now!)*

> Research shows:
> The more you know about something before you start to read it, the better you will understand it. Survey and Question will do this in less than five minutes.

READ

Read content area material slowly. If what you read does not make sense, it means that you might have read something wrong—REREAD.

HINT: *Sometimes it may be necessary to read something 4 or 5 times to understand it.*

RECITE

Summarize what you have read **aloud**. If you cannot retell it in your own words, it means that you did not understand it. REREAD. (It helps to take notes of the facts you have read. It will help you to study for a test later.)

HINT: *Just the act of writing will help you remember the material!*

REVIEW

Several days before a test, review your notes. Try to state the information in your own words. Have someone else ask you questions from your notes. (If you did all the other steps, this one should be the easy part!)

Research shows:
The more senses you use to study something, the better you will learn it. With SQ3R you are using seeing, hearing, speaking, and writing (touch).

UNIT 1: The Story of
THE NATIVE AMERICANS: The Indians

After surveying this story, I can tell that:

1. The term Native Americans refers to _____.
   a. the colonists   b. the Indians

2. The Indians who lived in the Southwest were the _____.
   a. Anasazis and Navajos   b. Algonquians and Iroquois

3. The Iroquois clans lived in homes called

   _____.

   a. longhouses   b. wigwams

After looking at the objective questions and constructed-response questions, I can tell that:

4. The time before Europeans came to America is called _____.
   a. colonial   b. prehistory

5 . The role of women in the Algonquian and Iroquois tribes was one of

   _____.

   a. slavery   b. importance

ANSWER BOX
1. The term Native Americans refers to the Indians.
2. The Indians who lived in the southwest were the Anasazis and Navajos.
3. The Iroquois clans lived in homes called longhouses.
4. The time before Europeans came to America is called prehistory.
5. The role of women in the Algonquian and Iroquois tribes was one of importance.

Read the following selection carefully. Stop after each section to retell the main idea in your own words.

The Story of The Native Americans: The Indians

★★

Scientists think that the first people to live in America came from Asia. They base this guess on the discovery of **fossils**. There certainly is no dry route there now. But people who study the earth know that there once was a **land bridge**. It crossed the **Bering Strait** from Asia to Alaska. This bridge existed during the last ice age, about **8,000 B.C.** Some people may have migrated long before that. The first Americans probably followed herds of buffalo. Perhaps something happened in Asia that caused them to leave.

Beringia land bridge from Asia to North America

INDIANS OF THE SOUTHWEST

Anasazi adobe houses and pottery

The Anasazi Indians

When the ice began to melt, the ocean covered the bridge. By that time, Indians lived all over North and South America. Quite a bit is known about the Indian tribes and nations. The Anasazi Indians lived in the Southwest for centuries before the Spanish came. Spanish explorers landed on the west coast in about 1500 A.D.

2

The Anasazis are the **ancestors** of the Pueblo people. They raised corn and squash on their farms. They hunted deer, rabbit and birds. The women wove the fibers of the yucca plants and turkey feathers into blankets.

People on "digs", who study the Anasazi villages, or pueblos, find pieces of pottery and baskets with beautiful designs. The early Indians liked lovely things.

The Anasazis lived in caves. Often the Indians built **adobe**, or clay, houses in front of the caves. They had no written language. They drew pictures on rocks to record important things. One of the carvings you can see today is of Mother Earth.

The Anasazi tribe had many gods. The Sun God, or Father, and Mother Earth were the most important. The Anasazi Indians wore masks during religious ceremonies. They danced so the gods would give them good crops, and good health.

The Navajo Indians

The **Navajo** Indians lived in the same area. They farmed, hunted and raised sheep. Religion was very important to them. Navajos tried to be at peace and harmony with Mother Earth at all times. "Walking in beauty," meant they were respecting and caring for all of nature. The Navajos used sand paintings in healing ceremonies. The Healer uses the sand painting to tell the story of the gods.

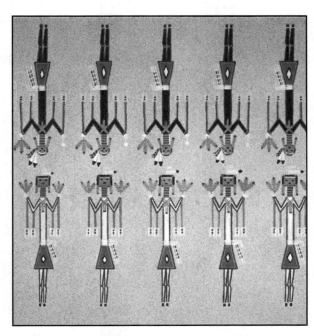

Humans and plants were usually part of Navajo sand paintings

There is no written record before the arrival of the Spanish. There is still much research to be done. For now, the time before the Europeans came is called **prehistory**.

INDIANS OF THE NORTHEAST

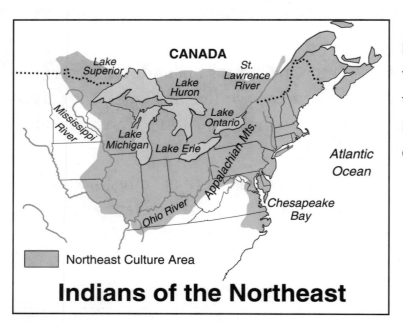

CANADA

Lake Superior

St. Lawrence River

Lake Huron

Mississippi River

Lake Ontario

Lake Michigan

Lake Erie

Appalachian Mts.

Atlantic Ocean

Ohio River

Chesapeake Bay

Northeast Culture Area

Indians of the Northeast

All the way across the continent, the Northeastern Woodland tribes made their homes. The **Algonquians** and the **Iroquois** greeted the Pilgrims from England when they landed in Massachusetts.

Forests of the Northeast provided for the needs of the Algonquians and Iroquois.

The Algonquians

A number of Indian tribes spoke the Algonquian language. They were the Pequot, Massachusett, Narraganset, and Powhatan tribes. The men hunted deer, trapped animals, and fished. They gathered various plant roots, seeds, wild rice and berries. The women were the farmers and even owned the land. During the warm weather, they walked or traveled in canoes made of birch bark. In the winter they used snowshoes and toboggans.

The Algonquians wore clothes made from animal skins. They lived in **wigwams**. These were tents made of poles, and covered with bark from the birch trees or animal skins.

4

The Iroquois

The Iroquois were a "nation" of Indians made up of five tribes. These were the Mohawk, Oneida, Onondaga, Cayuga and Seneca tribes. They lived in the eastern woodland, too. Today this is New York State. The Iroquois were skilled warriors. They considered the Algonquians their enemies, often fighting them. Some historians call them "savages" because they were so cruel to the people they captured. The five tribes fought each other, too. There seemed to be wars going on all the time. Finally, they joined together to become the "**League of the Five Nations**".

The Iroquois called themselves, the **People of the Longhouse**. Each **longhouse** was the home of a **clan**, several families related to each

Each clan of the Iroquois lived in a longhouse. The village was surrounded by a wall of pointed logs.

other. Each family had a small rectangle of space, about the size of a double door. The family lived on the ground level and stored their baskets, pots and animal skins on a platform above them. Two families cooked at the fires that were placed down the center aisle of the longhouse. The fires also gave light, because there were no windows. The Iroquois built walls around their villages for protection.

The men hunted deer with bows and arrows. They fished with nets and traps. Hollowed out tree trunks served as canoes. During the winter, they tapped maple trees to get syrup.

5

Village councils governed the Iroquois. Members of each clan would meet and make decisions about how to rule the village. Then **representatives** from all the villages would meet. They would make the laws to govern the entire Iroquois nation. It has been said that the men who wrote the United States Constitution studied the Iroquois system of government. It gave them valuable ideas about a good political system.

The head of each clan was a woman called the clan mother. Clan mothers picked the council leaders. All important council decisions had to be approved by the clan mothers. The women owned the longhouses and their contents.

THE FIRST NATIVE AMERICANS

The Spanish explorers met the Anasazis in the Southwest. Some say that the first school in the United States was built in New Mexico.

The Algonquians and the Iroquois were the tribes that met the settlers who came from England and began the first permanent settlements. These were the tribes that taught the New Englanders how to plant corn, beans and squash. They taught them to survive during the first harsh winters.

The Indians are the first **Native Americans**.

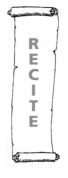

Name the four Native American groups discussed in this article. Tell where they lived and 3 facts about each of them.

TERMS TO REMEMBER The following Names, Dates, Places, and Words about The Native Americans are important to remember. Study them carefully. The sentences will help you understand their meanings.

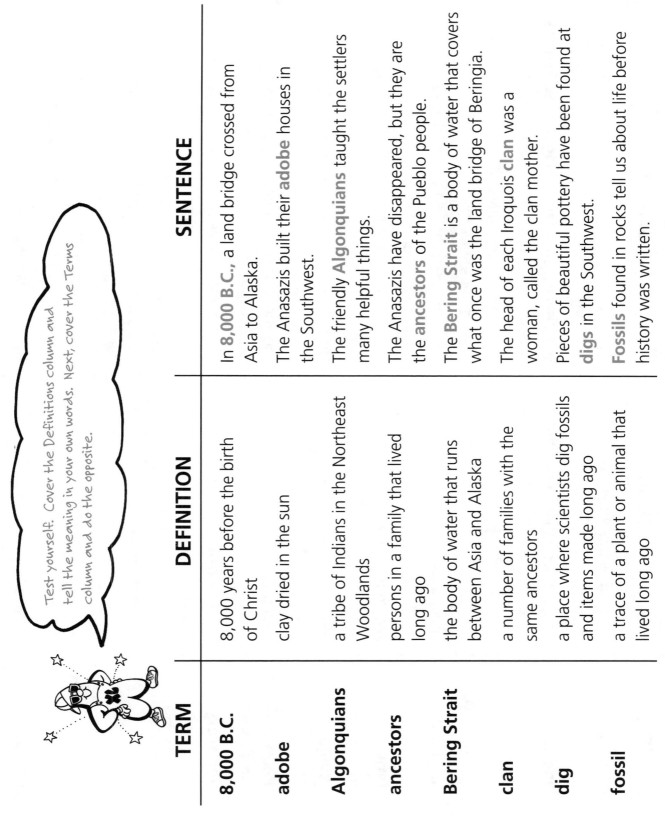

Test yourself. Cover the Definitions column and tell the meaning in your own words. Next, cover the Terms column and do the opposite.

TERM	DEFINITION	SENTENCE
8,000 B.C.	8,000 years before the birth of Christ	In **8,000 B.C.**, a land bridge crossed from Asia to Alaska.
adobe	clay dried in the sun	The Anasazis built their **adobe** houses in the Southwest.
Algonquians	a tribe of Indians in the Northeast Woodlands	The friendly **Algonquians** taught the settlers many helpful things.
ancestors	persons in a family that lived long ago	The Anasazis have disappeared, but they are the **ancestors** of the Pueblo people.
Bering Strait	the body of water that runs between Asia and Alaska	The **Bering Strait** is a body of water that covers what once was the land bridge of Beringia.
clan	a number of families with the same ancestors	The head of each Iroquois **clan** was a woman, called the clan mother.
dig	a place where scientists dig fossils and items made long ago	Pieces of beautiful pottery have been found at **digs** in the Southwest.
fossil	a trace of a plant or animal that lived long ago	**Fossils** found in rocks tell us about life before history was written.

TERM	DEFINITION	SENTENCE
Iroquois	tribes of Native Americans in the Northeast Woodlands	The **Iroquois** hunted deer in the forests of New York State.
land bridge	a strip of land that crosses the water between two land masses	Scientists believe a **land bridge**, called Beringia, once crossed the water between Asia and Alaska.
League of Five Nations	five tribes that joined together	The **League of Five Nations** vowed to keep peace among their tribes.
longhouse	large, bark-covered houses of the Iroquois	Fires were used for light and cooking in the windowless **longhouse**
Native Americans	People born in America	The Indians are the real **Native Americans**
Navajos	Native American tribes that cared for nature.	The **Navajos** respected and lived in the Southwest
"People of the Longhouse"	the Iroquois	The Iroquois were referred to as **"People of the Longhouse."**
prehistory	the time before there was a written language	In America the time before the Europeans came is called **prehistory**
representative	a person who speaks for a group of people at a meeting	**Representatives** from each Iroquois village would meet a to decide how to govern the Five Nations.
village council	a group that governed the Iroquois	A member of each clan met at the **village council** to make rules for the village.
warrior	a brave fighting man	The Iroquois were skilled **warriors**
wigwam	house of the Algonquians	The Algonquians bent thin tree trunks to give the **wigwams** their shape.

Objective Questions

Circle the correct answer choice for each question.

NEVER LEAVE A BLANK! It will almost always be marked wrong. Take an educated guess. Usually, you can eliminate two of the four answers. Then you have a 50-50 chance of getting it right. TRY!

1. The first people in America crossed a land bridge from:
   a. South America   b. Asia
   c. Europe   d. Antarctica

2. The Indians probably came to America:
   a. to find good weather   b. to find freedom
   c. to find food   d. to find neighbors

3. Why is the time before the Europeans came called "prehistory"?
   a. People did not live in America then. b. The records were lost.
   c. The people were nomads.   d. Native Americans did not
                                               have a written language.

4. Which word describes a group of tribes?
   a. neighborhood   b. community
   c. village   d. nation

5. The explorers who first explored the Southwest were from:
   a. England   b. Spain
   c. Holland   d. Mexico

6. The cave dwellers lived in towns called:
   a. yuccas   b. digs
   c. pueblos   d. adobes

★★★

7. Which conclusion should NOT be drawn?

   a. The Indians were always   b. The Indians knew how to grow crops.
       enemies of the settlers.

   c. The Iroquois lived in villages.   d. The Iroquois had a form of government.

8. What does the phrase, "walk in beauty" mean?

   a. Navajo people were very good looking.   b. Navajo people valued health.

   c. Navajo people valued nature.   d. Navajo people walked on nice days.

Base your answers to questions 9 through 11 on the picture below.

9. What does this picture show?
   a. a hogan   b. a wigwam
   c. a long house   d. a pueblo

★★★

10. Who lived in this type of house?
a. the Algonquians   b. the Iroquois
c. the Anasazis   d. the Navajos

11. What material probably covers this home?
a. reeds   b. clothe
c. grass   d. animal skins

---

12. How can we tell that women were important to the Algonquian and Iroquois tribes?
a. They owned property.   b. They were warriors.
c. They gathered food.   d. They knew the settlers.

13. Which statement best explains the government of the Iroquois Nation?
a. They obeyed the laws of England.
b. Warriors kept the groups together.
c. Representatives from each village met to make laws.
d. The tribes were relatives.

14. Why did the Indian tribes throughout North America have such different houses?
a. They each wanted to be unique.
b. They learned different styles from the Europeans.
c. They each used the natural resources in their area.
d. They were unable to communicate.

15. Which Native American flag is pictured here?
a. the flag of the Algonquians
b. the flag of the Navajos
c. the flag of the Five Nations
d. the flag of the Anasazi tribe

Constructed-Response Questions

Write your answers to the questions that follow in the spaces provided.

Constructed Response questions often require you to use information you already know as well as the data given. Think about what you have learned as you answer each question. (Questions 5 through 9 in this section are examples.)

Base your answers to questions 1 through 4 on the picture below:

Native Americans from the Northeastern Woodlands

1. How are these Native Americans hollowing out the tree?

_____

_____

_____

2. What are they making?

_____

_____

Constructed-Response Questions

3. What will it be used for?

_____

_____

4. How are the people in this picture working together?

_____

_____

The Algonquians and the Iroquois were both Indian groups in the Northeast. Fill in the chart below to describe them.

Tribe	Homes	Food	Transportation	Role of Women
Algonquians	**5.** _____	- hunted & trapped Animals - fished - ate plant roots	**6.** _____	farmers **7.** _____
Iroquois	longhouses	- hunted **8.** _____ **9.** _____	canoes of hollowed tree trunks	- clan mother - overseer of governing council

★★

Mary Jemison, age 13, had been captured by Indians in the 1750's. This is how she described her life to James Seaver, an interviewer, many years later. Base your answers to questions 10 through 12 on her statement:

"Being now settled and provided with a home, I was employed in nursing the children, and doing light work about the house. Occasionally, I was sent with the Indian hunters when they went but a short distance, to help them carry their game (animals.) My situation was easy: I had no particular hardships to endure (face.) But still, the recollection (memory) of my parents, my brothers and sisters, my home, and my own captivity, destroyed my happiness, and made me constantly solitary (alone), lonesome, and gloomy. My [Indian] sisters would not allow me to speak English in their hearing." (Simplified)

10. Why did Mary think that her "situation was easy"?

_____

_____

_____

_____

_____

_____

_____

11. How did Mary feel about her new life?

_____

_____

_____

12. Why do you think the Indians didn't want her to speak English?

_____

_____

_____

14

★★

UNIT 2: The Story of
THE 13 COLONIES

After surveying the story, I can tell that:

1. The first permanent English colony in North America was
_____.

   a. Plymouth, Massachusetts   b. Jamestown, Virginia

2. The Dutch colony of New Amsterdam is now known as
_____.

   a. New Jersey   b. New York City

3. The colony of Rhode Island was created for _____.
   a. fur and fishing   b. religious freedom

After looking at the objective questions and constructed-response questions, I can tell that:

4. All of the 13 original colonies were located along the _____.
   a. Atlantic coast   b. James River

5. The phrase "city of the brotherly love" refers to _____.
   a. Boston   b. Philadelphia

ANSWER BOX

1. The first permanent English colony in North America was Jamestown, Virginia.
2. The dutch colony of New Amsterdam is now known as New York City.
3. The colony of rhode Island was created for religious freedom.
4. All of the 13 original colonies were located along the Atlantic coast.
5. The phrase "city of brotherly love" refers to Philadelphia.

Read the following selection carefully. Stop after each section to retell the main idea in your own words.

The Story of The Thirteen Colonies

★★★

In the early 1600s, many people were not satisfied with their lives in Europe. For a number of reasons, they decided to leave their homes. They hoped for opportunities in the New World.

There were big differences among the thirteen **colonies**. The best way to understand them is to know why the people came, and where they settled. Settlements did not start in one spot and then spread out. One colony began in the warm South. The next colony started in the colder climate of the North. Soon, as more and more people arrived, the spaces between the colonies were filled in, 13 in number. It is probably easiest to look at them in the order of the dates they arrived.

Virginia

In **1607**, three ships arrived at the Virginia coast after months at sea. These brave English people sailed up the James River. There they founded the village of **Jamestown**. The river and the village were named after King James of England. The colonists considered themselves Englishmen. They honored the same laws as they always had.

Jamestown, Virginia: First permanent English colony in North America.

These colonists arrived with dreams of finding gold and riches in the new land. There were "gentlemen" aboard. They had lived the lives of the very rich. So they knew nothing about real work. The others had skills. But none of them knew how to survive in the new land. Money could not help them.

16

At first they built a town of mud huts. However, hunger, disease, and Indian attacks killed almost everyone. Of the five hundred colonists in Jamestown, only 60 lived through the winter of 1609. Then help arrived from **England**. Jamestown, the first colony in North America survived.

The settlers learned about the forests and the land. The colony prospered. In 1612, John Rolfe began to grow tobacco. Rolfe later married **Pocahontas**, the daughter of an Indian chief. This made peace between the colonists and the Indians.

People in Europe wanted to buy plenty of tobacco. However, it took many workers to raise a crop. By 1619, **slaves** were brought to Virginia. The farmers bought them to use as free labor. Slaves worked on their land and in their homes. The southern climate was perfect for farming. Small farms quickly grew into large **plantations**. Houses had shaded porches and a separate building for the kitchen. Virginia was very hot during the long summers.

Massachusetts

Another ship, the Mayflower, left England for Virginia in **1620**. A terrible storm blew them northward. They landed in Massachusetts instead. These were the **Pilgrims**, or **Puritans**, who wanted **religious freedom**. While on board, the Pilgrims drew up the **Mayflower Compact**. This was an agreement among all of them. Their new

First Sermon at Plymouth

land would be ruled by the will of most of the people. They built villages, with the church in the center of town. The Pilgrims built houses made of wood with thatched, or mud and grass, roofs. During the winter, the great fireplace was kept going all day. Winter was long and harsh in the North.

Friendly Indians taught the Pilgrims how to clear the land. They introduced the settlers to new foods. Farming in the rocky soil was not easy. But deer and turkey were plentiful in the woods.

The Puritans had very strict religious rules. They soon forgot that they had come to the New World to be able to worship in their own way. They did not accept those who would not follow their way of life. Some people felt they had not found the religious freedom they had come for.

Rhode Island

Roger Williams: his belief in religious freedom led to the founding of Rhode Island.

Roger Williams was driven out of Massachusetts for his beliefs. Rogers, a minister, walked south alone. He bought land from the Narragansett Indians in 1635. His colony, Rhode Island, welcomed people with different religious views. It became successful at fishing.

New Hampshire

Just to the north of Massachusetts, New Hampshire was established in 1623. Settlers were moving to new areas very quickly. Most of those living here traded furs or fished for a living. The mountains were covered with pine and oak trees. These would soon provide wood to build ships for American fishermen.

Connecticut

As they began to know the land better, others traveled south. They came upon wonderful farmland. In 1638, these colonists established Connecticut. At this point, they were moving onto Indian land. There was a fierce war. Many were killed on both sides. The Indians destroyed many New England towns. Finally, the Indians surrendered.

The colonies of Massachusetts, Rhode Island, New Hampshire, and Connecticut became known as the **New England Colonies**. The settlers of each of them had come from England. Their colonial government and customs were based on those of England.

New Amsterdam was later renamed New York City.

New York

Meanwhile, **Dutch** colonists settled at the mouth of the **Hudson River**. They named their town **New Amsterdam**. Many of the Dutch sailed up the Hudson. The fertile, or rich, land was turned into large farms. In 1666, the English Navy sailed into the harbor. That ended the Dutch reign.

New Amsterdam was renamed New York. It was a natural **port**. Businessmen and craftsmen opened stores. They provided goods for all the colonies. Fishing fleets and ships, loaded with cloth, pots and pans, and even guns, arrived in the New York harbor. It became a busy center of trade. Banks and a stock market were opened in this growing financial center.

New Jersey

Across the Hudson from New York, the British claimed an area. The **Duke of York** named it New Jersey. Free land was offered to attract settlers. The promise of freedom of worship brought **Quakers** from the countries of Ireland, Scotland and Wales. Other colonists from New England came down, too. They found the land to be good for farming.

19

Pennsylvania

The Quaker **William Penn** founded Pennsylvania. This large colony was to the west of New Jersey. Penn insisted that there be religious freedom throughout Pennsylvania. The Pennsylvania Dutch settled there. They operated huge farms in the area. This cultural group was free to live and worship without fear. Quakers came from Europe for religious reasons, too. The Quakers paid the Indians good prices for their land. The Quakers and Indians lived in peace in Pennsylvania.

Colonists from Sweden built the first log cabins there. These were wooden logs, placed on top of each other and held together with mud and grass.

William Penn planned the bustling city of **Philadelphia**. Its name means "the city of brotherly love." Benjamin Franklin left Boston to start a newspaper here.

Maryland

Maryland became a colony of rich tobacco fields and busy villages. It lies just north of Virginia. For hundreds of years there had been trouble between Catholics and Protestants in England. King Charles gave Maryland to Lord Baltimore, a Catholic. In 1633, a ship carrying about 200 passengers left England. Both Catholics and Protestants were on board, as well as two Catholic priests. Maryland became a colony where Catholics could practice their religion. Catholics and Protestants lived and worked side by side.

Delaware

A little snip of land on Maryland's coast was the colony of Delaware. Swedish settlers started the colony in 1638. They called it New Sweden. However, within 20 years, the British took over the colony. Then there was a big quarrel. Pennsylvania wanted the Delaware River. It had no other way out to the sea. Maryland wanted Delaware because it was attached to their land. This argument went on until the American

Revolution. Then Delaware declared itself free from any other colony and free from England.

The colonies of New York, New Jersey, Pennsylvania, Maryland, and Delaware were home to people with varied cultures. They made up the **Middle Atlantic Colonies**.

The Carolinas

On the map, skip over Virginia, which we've already mentioned. Just south of that colony, were North and South Carolina. Settlers looking for farmland kept going farther south. Rice and tobacco were crops that grew well in Carolina soil. Soon farms grew into plantations. Slaves provided labor here, too.

Georgia

Georgia lies just under South Carolina. This was a special colony. **James Oglethorpe** was a member of the English Parliament. He visited a friend in prison. Conditions in English prisons were terrible. Oglethorpe realized many of the prisoners had not done awful things. Most of them owed money. But they could not pay back the money without work. They would be in prison for life. He convinced Parliament those people

Tobacco Farm

needed a second chance. In 1732, prisoners and very poor people got passage to Georgia. There they received a small farm and a chance for a new life. Georgia became the last of the thirteen colonies.

You can guess that Virginia, North Carolina, South Carolina, and Georgia were called the Southern Colonies. Their common interest was farming.

By 1770 more than 2 million people lived in England's 13 North American colonies. By 1776 the drums of freedom were rolling. The thirteen colonies would become the thirteen states of the United States of America.

The 13 Colonies in 1750

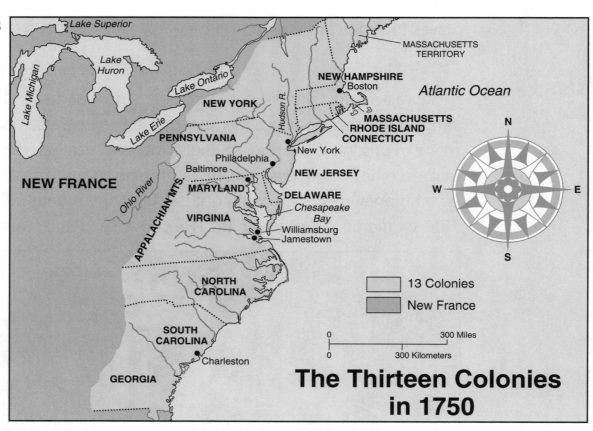

The Thirteen Colonies in 1750

RECITE

Name the thirteen colonies. Tell one important fact about each colony.

TERMS TO REMEMBER The following Names, Dates, Places, and Words about The Thirteen Colonies are important to remember. Study them carefully. The sentences will help you understand their meanings.

Test yourself. Cover the Definitions column and tell the meaning in your own words. Next, cover the Terms column and do the opposite.

TERM	DEFINITION	SENTENCE
1607	The year the English landed in Virginia	Three British ships arrived in Virginia in **1607**, after three months at sea.
1620	The Pilgrims land in Massachusetts	A storm swept the Pilgrims northward and they landed in Massachusetts in **1620**
colony	A place that is ruled by another country	The Pilgrims built a **colony** in a new country, but were still governed by England.
Duke of York	Brother of the King of England	The English changed the name of New Amsterdam in honor of the **Duke of York**
Dutch	People from Holland or the Netherlands	The **Dutch** sailed from Holland to farm along the Hudson River.
England	A country in Europe, also called Great Britain	The Pilgrims, or Puritans, left **England** to find religious freedom.
Europe	A continent	The first American settlers came from countries in **Europe**

23

TERM	DEFINITION	SENTENCE
Hudson River	A river in New York State	The Dutch sailed up the Hudson River from New York City to farm the fertile land.
Jamestown, Virginia	The first English settlement in the New World	Hunger, disease, and Indian attacks killed almost everyone in the Jamestown colony.
Mayflower Compact	A written agreement made on board the Mayflower	The Pilgrims drew up the Mayflower Compact agreeing that the new colony would be ruled by the will of most of the people.
Middle Atlantic Colonies	New York, New Jersey, Pennsylvania, Delaware, and Maryland	The Middle Atlantic colonies lie between New England and the Southern colonies.
New Amsterdam	The Dutch name for New York City	The Dutch built a city at the mouth of the Hudson River and named it New Amsterdam.
New England Colonies	Massachusetts, New Hampshire, Rhode Island, and Connecticut	People from England started all the New England colonies.
North America	A continent—Europeans called it the "New World"	The United States is one of the countries located on the continent of North America
James Oglethorpe	The founder of the colony of Georgia	James Oglethorpe arranged for English prisoners to settle in Georgia.
William Penn	The founder of Pennsylvania	William Penn insisted on religious freedom for all who lived in Pennsylvania.
Philadelphia, Pennsylvania	A city planned by William Penn	The name Philadelphia means "brotherly love."
Pilgrims or Puritans	People who left England for religious reasons	The Pilgrims or Puritans, had very strict religious rules.

TERM	DEFINITION	SENTENCE
plantation	A large farm	The plantation owners in the South used slaves to grow cotton.
Plymouth, Massachusetts	The second colony settled in America	A storm swept the Mayflower to Plymouth, Massachusetts, a spot far north of Virginia.
Pocahontas	The daughter of an Indian Chief in Virginia	The marriage of Pocahontas and John Rolfe brought peace to Virginia.
port	A harbor	New York was a natural port because ships could travel in and out easily.
Quakers	A religious group	The Quakers, a religious group, paid the Indians for their land.
Religious Freedom	Freedom of worship	Every American has religious freedom, the right to practice his or her own religion.
settlement	A colony in a new region	As more people came, settlements spread up and down the Atlantic coast.
slaves	A person who is owned by another person	People brought slaves to work for free.
Southern Colonies	Virginia, North Carolina, South Carolina, and Georgia	The warm climate in the Southern Colonies made it a good place to raise tobacco.
Roger Williams	A minister banished from Massachusetts	Roger Williams paid the Indians for land on which to build his colony of Rhode Island.

Objective Questions

Circle the correct answer choice for each question.

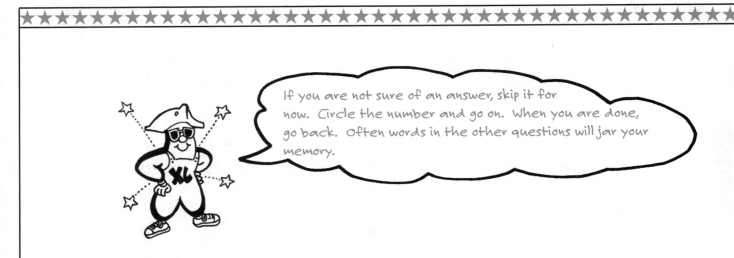

If you are not sure of an answer, skip it for now. Circle the number and go on. When you are done, go back. Often words in the other questions will jar your memory.

1. The Mayflower Contract was important because:
   a. Massachusetts was the most important colony in America.
   b. It was a religious document.
   c. It was an agreement with the Indians.
   d. It set up the first self-government in America.

2. The colony first settled by the Dutch was:
   a. New Jersey   b. New York
   c. Delaware   d. Maryland

3. When a person is able to attend any church or synagogue he or she pleases, it is called:
   a. academic freedom   b. religious freedom
   c. freedom of speech   d. freedom of the press

4. All of the 13 original colonies were located:
   a. East of the Appalachian Mountains   b. North of present day Canada
   c. East of the Atlantic Ocean   d. West of the Pacific Ocean.

5. The term, "the 1600's" refers to which of the following:
   a. one year   b. a decade
   c. one hundred years   d. one thousand years

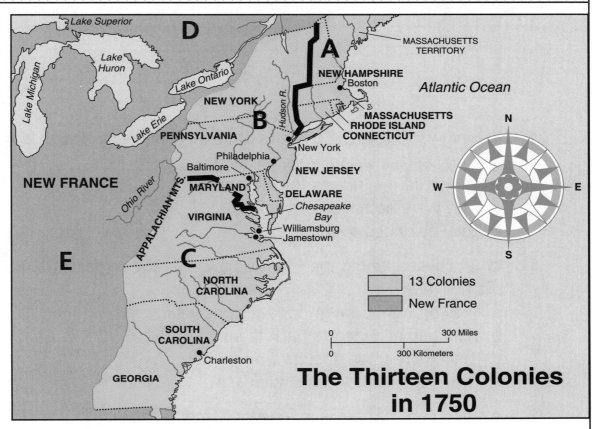

The 13 Colonies in 1750

The Thirteen Colonies in 1750

13 Colonies
New France

0 — 300 Miles
0 — 300 Kilometers

Examine the map of the 13 colonies to answer question 6 through 10:

6. Which letter on the map above shows the Middle Colonies?
a. C   b. E
c. D   d. B

7. Which letter shows the Southern Colonies?
a. E   b. C
c. D   d. A

8. Which letter shows the New England Colonies?
a. A   b. D
c. C   d. B

9. Which letter shows a part of the U.S. today that was not an English colony?
a. D   b. A
c. E   d. C

Objective Questions

10. Which letter is not a part of our country today?
   a. B
   b. D
   c. E
   d. A

_____

11. In what way were the colonies of Pennsylvania and Rhode Island alike?
   a. They used slaves to work the land.
   b. They paid the Indians for the land.
   c. They were both Catholic colonies.
   d. They belonged to the French.

12. What advantage did the Pilgrims have that the settlers in Jamestown did not have?
   a. They brought enough food for one year.
   b. They had rich men to back them.
   c. There were three doctors among them.
   d. They got help from the Indians.

13. A settlement of people in a new country is called:
   a. a democracy
   b. a cultural group
   c. a new nation
   d. a colony

14. All of the following statements are true EXCEPT:
   a. All the American colonies permitted religious freedom.
   b. Most of the new colonies were settled by the English.
   c. The colony of Georgia was settled by former prisoners.
   d. The Jamestown colony was almost wiped out in its first winter.

15. Philadelphia is called "the city of brotherly love." What made this so?
   a. William Penn accepted people of all religions.
   b. It was the first planned city in America.
   c. Colonists from Sweden lived there.
   d. Benjamin Franklin moved to Philadelphia.

Constructed-Response Questions

Write your answers to the questions that follow in the spaces provided.

★★★

> Some constructed response questions are comprehension questions. The answer is found directly in the data provided. Read carefully. (This is true for some of the documents in this section!)

Carefully study the picture. Then answer questions 1 through 3 below:

The Pilgrims landed on Plymouth Rock, Massachusetts on December 11, 1620.

1. What type of boat did the Pilgrims use to cross the Atlantic Ocean? How was it powered? Why was this a problem?

_____

_____

2. What season of the year did they land? Was the weather a help or a hindrance?

_____

3. What do you think their most immediate tasks need be? Why?

_____

_____

★★★

Constructed-Response Questions

Read the poem, "First Thanksgiving." Then answer questions 4 through 7 below.

First Thanksgiving

Three days we had
        feasting, praying, singing
Three days outdoors at wooden tables,
Colonists and Indians together,
Celebrating a full harvest,
A golden summer of corn.

    We hunted the woods, finding
    Venison, deer and wild turkey.

    We brought our plump geese and ducks,
    Great catches of silver fish.

    We baked corn meal bread with nuts
    Journey cake, and steaming succotash.

    We roasted the meat on pits
    Before huge, leaping fires.

    We stewed our tawny pumpkins
    In buckets of bubbling maple sap

Three days we had
        feasting, praying, singing

Three days outdoors at wooden tables,
Colonists and Indians together,
Celebrating a full harvest,
Praying, each to our God.

Myra Cohn Livingston

4. Who took part in the celebration?

_____

_____

5. Why were they celebrating?

_____

_____

6. Where and when did this scene probably take place?

_____

_____

7. How did they get the foods they ate?

_____

_____

Constructed-Response Questions

Review the passenger list for the English ship, *Hopewell*. Then answer questions 1 to 12 below.

8. When was the ship leaving London and where was it headed?

_____

_____

_____

9. How many passengers were on board?

_____

_____

10. Did the colonial people bring their children to the New World? How can you tell?

_____

_____

_____

11. Who as bringing his servant to America? How can you tell?

_____

_____

Hopewell   1 April, 1635

In the Hopewell of London
William Bundocke, Mr. for New England

Jo. Cooper	41 of Oney, in Buckinghamsire
Edmond Farrington	47 of Oney, in Buckingham sire
William Parryer	36 of Olney, in Buckingham sire
Geo. Griggs	42 of Landen in Buckingham
Philip Kyrtland	21 of Sherington in Buckingham
Nath Kyrtland	19 in Buckingham
Children of George Griggs, aforesaid	
Thomas Griggs	13
William Griggs	14
Eliza Griggs	10
Mary Griggs	6
Janet Griggs	2
Wibroe wife of John Cooper	42 years
Eliza wife of Edward Farrington	49
Alyce wife of William Parryer	37
Alyce wife of George Griggs	42
children of John Cooper, aforesaid	
Mary Cooper	13
Jo. Cooper	10
Thomas Cooper	7
Martha Cooper	5
Phillip Phillipp, servt to Jo. Cooper	15 years
children of Edw. Farrington	
Sarra Farrington	14
Mathew Farrington	12
Jo. Farrington	11
Eliza Farrington	8
Mary Parryer	7

_____

12. Why do you think there were no people over 50-years-old on the trip?

_____

_____

DBQ I

DOCUMENT-BASED QUESTION

Directions: The task below is based on documents 1 through 6. It will test your ability to work with historical documents as well as your knowledge of social studies. Study each document, and answer the questions that follow. They will help you to organize your essay.

Historical Background:

Relations between the colonists and Native Americans were mixed. Although they traded with each other, they often did not get along. Fights, and even wars, sometimes broke out.

Task:

Part A is made up of short-answer questions. <u>After reading the essay question below</u>, answer each question fully. Use the information in the documents and your knowledge of social studies for your answers.

Essay Question:

Describe the relationship between the colonists and the Native Americans. In your essay be sure to include:

• What they traded.

• Why they often did not get along.

• What each group did to try to make things better.

Document-Based Question

Part A—Short-Answer Questions

Directions: Study each document, and answer the questions that follow. Base your answers on the documents provided as well as your knowledge of social studies.

DOCUMENT 1

Captain John Smith trading tools for corn with the Native Americans.

TRADE VALUES

For Trade by Indians:		For Trade by Colonists:
2 beaver skin	=	3 metal knives
1 beaver skin	=	25 loads of gun powder
1 beaver skin	=	1-gallon metal cooking pot
1 beaver skin	=	1 1/2 yards of calico cloth

Study the picture and the Trade Values above. Then answer the following questions.

33

★★

1. What did the Indians want from the colonists?

_____

_____

_____

_____

Why?

_____

_____

_____

2. What did the colonists want from the Indians?

_____

_____

_____

_____

Why?

_____

_____

_____

3. How can you tell there was distrust between the two groups?

_____

_____

_____

_____

★★

Document-Based Question

DOCUMENT 2

Fighting and even wars often occurred between the colonists and the Native Americans.

1. Describe the weapons of the Indians.

_____

_____

_____

2. Describe the weapons of the colonists.

_____

_____

_____

3. What has happened to the colonial village?

_____

_____

Document-Based Question

DOCUMENT 3

Dutch Officer, Peter Minuit, buying Manhattan Island in New York from the Indians. The Dutch paid about $24.00 in beads and other items.

1. Based on this picture, what did the Dutch trade for the island of Manhattan?

_____

_____

_____

2. Do you think this was a fair trade? Explain.

_____

_____

_____

_____

Document-Based Question

DOCUMENT 4

Lion Gardiner lived on Long Island, New York, in the 1600s. The passage below is from his journal. It tells of a conversation he had with a local Indian. In it the Indian says:

> ...our fathers had plenty of deer and skins, our plains were full of deer, as our woods, and of turkeys, and our coves full of fish and fowl (birds). But these English having gotten our land, they with long knives cut down the grass, and with axes chop down the trees; their cows and horses eat the grass, and their hogs spoil our clam banks, and we shall all be starved....

Excerpts from Lion Gardiner's Journal (simplified)

1. What did the Indians think of their lives before the settlers came?

_____

_____

_____

2. What problems did they have because of the settlers?

_____

_____

_____

3. What were the Indians afraid of?

_____

_____

_____

37

Document-Based Question

DOCUMENT 5

A settler from Jamestown, Virginia, wrote about his dealings with the Indians. Here is part of what he said:

> The Indians had made a treaty with the King of England. This treaty lasted for quite a while so that our people began to trust them. The savages (Indians) became so friendly that they often visited the English (colonists) and dined with them in their homes. They even offered to exchange furs, fish and other things with them. But this was nothing but a trick. The Indians only waited for a good chance to kill all the English.
>
> On the day of the killing, some of the savages visited our people, eating with them in their homes. At a given signal, they drew their weapons and killed 347 of the surprised English.
>
> There are different opinions about the reason for this bloody attack.... My opinion is that their priests, who are tools of the devil, made them believe that the English had come to destroy them. The attack was made to prevent this.

From: First Hand Accounts of Virginia 1575–1705; The Indian Massacre of 1622 (simplified)

1. This colonist referred to the Indians as "savages." What does that tell about how the colonists felt toward the Indians?

   _____

   _____

   _____

2. According to this story, why didn't the Indians trust the English?

   _____

   _____

3. Why didn't the English trust the Indians?

   _____

   _____

Document-Based Question

DOCUMENT 6

The Duke of York set up laws for the New York colonists. The four laws below were meant to protect their Native American neighbors.

Indian Affairs

A. No purchase of lands from Indians shall be made without permission from the Governor. Also the buyer shall bring the Sachem (Indian) owner of such land before the Governor. He must state that he is satisfied with the payment made for his land. Only after this will the purchase be lawful.

B. All harm done to the Indians will be brought to Court. The Indians will be treated the same as if the problem had been between white man and white man.

C. No person shall sell, give, or trade any guns, gun powder, or bullets to any Indian without permission from the Governor.

D. The English and all others shall keep their cattle from destroying the Indians' corn in any ground where they have a right to plant.

From: The Duke of York's Laws 1665–75 (simplified)

1. How do you think the Indians were probably treated before these laws? Explain.

_____

_____

2. When a colonist bought land from an Indian, BOTH of them had to go to the governor's office. Why?

_____

_____

3. Why do you think the governor wanted to control the sale of guns to the Indians?

_____

_____

4. Why was it smart of the governor to protect the Indians?

_____

39

Document-Based Question

Part B—Essay

Directions: Review the documents in Part A and your answers. They will help you to write the essay below.

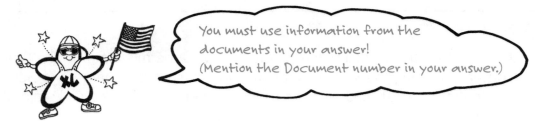

You must use information from the documents in your answer!
(Mention the Document number in your answer.)

Historical Background:

Relations between the colonists and Native Americans were mixed. Although they traded with each other, they often did not get along. Fights, and even wars, sometimes broke out.

Task:

Use the documents in Part A, your answers, and your knowledge of social studies to write the essay below.

Essay Question:

Describe the relationship between the colonists and the Native Americans. In your essay be sure to include:

- What they traded.

- Why they often did not get along.

- What each group did to try to make things better.

Use the graphic organizer on the next page to organize your answer!

40

GRAPHIC ORGANIZER

I started you off!

What they traded

Doc.	Notes
3	Indians gave Colonists:
1	- land (ex. Manhattan)
	-Corn
	-
	-
1	Colonists gave Indians:
1	- tools
	-beads
	-
	-

Why they did not get along

Doc.	Notes
4	Indians thought white men ruined their land:
	- cut down trees
	-
	-
	-
5	White men did not trust Indians' word:
	-
	-

What each did to make things better

Doc.	Notes
5	Indians made treaty with King of England
6	Duke of York made laws to protect Indians. Said:
	-
	-
	-

*There's more!
Look through the documents!*

41

Document-Based Question

Student Response

Use the information in your graphic organizer to write a detailed essay.

My suggestions below may help.

Introduction:
Restate the Historical Background <u>in your own words</u> as a start.

_____
_____
_____
_____
_____
_____

Add a transition sentence, such as "This essay will show..."

_____
_____
_____
_____
_____

Body: Put your notes into complete sentences. Add details. It helps to use one paragraph for each topic

_____
_____
_____
_____
_____
_____

Conclusion:
Summarize the ideas you presented. For example, "Therefore..." or "In summary..."

_____
_____
_____
_____
_____

42

Document-Based Question

★★★

UNIT 3: The Story of
THE REVOLUTIONARY WAR

After surveying the story, I can tell that:

1. The Revolutionary War started with _____.
  a. the Battle of Lexington and Concord
  b. the Boston Tea Party

2. The Revolutionary War ended at _____.
  a. Yorktown, Virginia   b. New York City

3. One major problem between the colonists and England was about _____.

  a. supplies
  b. taxes

After looking at the objective questions and constructed-response questions, I can tell that:

4. Patrick Henry was a great American _____.
  a. general
  b. speaker

5. The Revolutionary War was fought _____.
  a. in the late 1700s   b. in the early 1800s

ANSWER BOX
1. The Revolutionary War started with the Battle of Lexington and Concord.
2. The Revolutionary War ended at Yorktown, Virginia.
3. One major problem between the colonists and England was about taxes.
4. Patrick Henry was a great American speaker.
5. The Revolutionary War was fought in the late 1700s.

Read the following selection carefully. Stop after each section to retell the main idea in your own words.

★★★

The Story of The Revolutionary War

★★★

New Taxes Lead to Problems With England

The French and Indian War between France and England began in 1754. It lasted seven years. The war got its name because the Indians fought on the side of the French. The two countries were fighting for control of much of North America. Of course, the colonists fought for England.

When England won, King George of England and the British **Parliament** needed money to pay for the French and Indian War. They wanted the colonists to help pay for the war. The King charged taxes on almost everything to raise money. Tea was a favorite drink in the colonies. The tax on tea made the cost go up. Then the **British** came up with the **Stamp Act**. Every book, newspaper, and magazine had to bear a tax stamp. People in all of the colonies became very angry.

No Taxation Without Representation

The colonists worked hard in a new land. They did not want to buy goods from England for high prices. The colonists wanted to send a person to Parliament. He would explain their ideas. They wanted this representative to have a vote. The colonists wrote letters to **King George** and Parliament complaining about the taxes.

Back in England, the government ignored them. Laws just became stricter. British troops came to enforce the tax laws. The colonists in Boston were forced to have the soldiers live in their homes. This was known as the **Quartering Act**.

The call, "No taxation without representation" spread through the colonies. Many colonists began to think they should no longer be an English colony. They were known as the "**Patriots**." But a number of colonists thought that the colonies should be loyal to their Mother

Country. They wanted to remain part of England. They were called the "**Loyalists**," or "**Tories**." During the Revolutionary War, some of them acted as spies for the English.

The Boston Massacre

In 1770, a crowd of angry colonists in Boston threw snowballs at a British guard. Other soldiers came to help him. Soon they were fighting. The soldiers fired into the crowd. Four colonists were killed. The Patriots called this the "Boston Massacre." After that, things got even worse. The King sent over more troops. The tax on tea remained.

The Boston Tea Party

One night in December of that same year, Massachusetts's patriots dressed up like Mohawk Indians. They boarded the British ships. Soon crates of valuable tea floated in Boston Harbor. Ever since, this has been known as "**The Boston Tea Party**".

British troops fired at colonists, killing four of them. This was the Boston Massacre.

The Minutemen

Secretly, the colonists in Massachusetts formed a **militia**. These volunteers never had training. But they had to defend their land. These were the "**Minute Men**." They were ready for battle at a minute's notice.

The Battle of Lexington and Concord: Start of a War

In April 1775, **Paul Revere** heard that the British planned to attack Lexington. This town was across the river from Boston. The British thought the colonists had hidden ammunition there. Revere had a friend in Boston. This patriot waved a light from the tower of the North Church. The signal told Revere that the British troops had started for Lexington. Revere rode his horse all night. He let all the Minute Men know of the danger.

Outnumbered, the Minutemen fight the British at Lexington and Concord

When the British arrived in Lexington, the Minute Men surprised them. Although the colonists fought hard, the British won this battle. Then the troops headed for the town of Concord. When they came to the bridge in town, more Minute Men appeared. This time the British lost so many men, they had to run away. The Revolutionary War actually began then with "**the shot heard around the world**."

The Declaration of Independence

Just as the fighting began, colonial leaders held a meeting in Philadelphia. This first **Continental Congress** had to decide what to do. They asked the King of England to stop the attacks. He did not listen.

By July 4, 1776, **Thomas Jefferson** had written the Declaration of Independence. Representatives from all the colonies signed this statement. It declared that the colonies would be an independent country.

Representatives from the colonies sign the Declaration of Independence

This was a brave decision. England had a fine navy and a large army. The colonists were not soldiers and had no training.

The colonists did have some advantages, though. They had fought Indians in the woods. They hunted for much of their food. Under General George Washington's command, they learned to become soldiers. The British had been taught to fight in straight lines on open fields. They also wore bright red jackets. This made them easy targets for the colonists, who called them "**Red Coats**."

Both Sides Want New York

George Washington said that everything must be done to keep New York. He knew how badly the British wanted it. The side that controlled this region would probably win the war. If the British got New York, it would be easy for them to send supplies to their troops. They

**The Battle of Saratoga in New York
on October 17, 1777**

could go from New England to Pennsylvania to the southern colonies without any trouble. The harbor in New York City would receive supplies from England. British war ships could come and go with no one to stop them. The British did win New York City and Long Island.

Many of the important battles of the Revolutionary War were fought in New York. The British were winning. Then the colonists won the **Battle of Saratoga**, in New York. This was the turning point of the war. Benjamin Franklin had been hard at work in France. He tried to get the French to send aid to the colonies. The Battle of Saratoga convinced the French that the **Continental Army** could win the war. In 1777, France became an **ally**. They sent money and soldiers, led by **Lafayette**.

49

General George Washington in New York City

The British Surrender at Yorktown, Virginia

In **1781**, the Americans and French under General George Washington trapped the British. The British General Cornwallis surrendered at **Yorktown, Virginia**. This marked the end of the Revolutionary War.

The British had occupied New York City for many years. In 1783, when the last **Red Coat** left the city, George Washington said farewell to his officers at **Fraunces Tavern**. It is still a famous landmark in New York City. Washington was happy the war had ended. The colonies were free and independent and he was going home.

General Washington did not spend much time at his home in Mount Vernon. The new nation unanimously chose him to be the first President of the United States on April 30, **1789**.

R
E
C
I
T
E

Describe the main events that led up to the Revolutionary War. Explain why the untrained colonists managed to beat the powerful English army and navy.

TERMS TO REMEMBER The following Names, Dates, Places, and Words about The Revolutionary War are important to remember. Study them carefully. The sentences will help you understand their meanings.

Test yourself. Cover the Definitions column and tell the meaning in your own words. Next, cover the Terms column and do the opposite.

TERM	DEFINITION	SENTENCE
1781	The year the Revolutionary War was over	The Americans won the Battle of Yorktown in **1781**, ending the Revolutionary War.
1789	The first President chosen	The new nation selected George Washington as its first President in **1789**
ally	Friend, helper	The Indians were France's ally in the French and Indian War.
Battle of Lexington and Concord	The beginning of the Revolutionary War	The Minutemen fought the British in **Lexington and Concord** The Revolutionary War had begun.
Battle of Saratoga	The turning point of the war	Winning the **Battle of Saratoga** showed that the colonists could win the war.
Boston Massacre	British soldiers fire at citizens in Boston	The **Boston Massacre** happened in 1770, when British soldiers shot into a crowd and killed four patriots.
Boston Tea Party	Patriots dump teas overboard.	Angry patriots, dressed as Indians, tossed crates of tea into the Boston Harbor.

TERM	DEFINITION	SENTENCE
Britain	The name for England and all its colonies	Settlers from **Britain** founded the first American colonies.
Continental Army	The American Army	The **Continental Army**, led by General George Washington, fought the war for independence.
Continental Congress	The meeting of leaders from each colony	The **Continental Congress** met to decide how to deal with England..
General Cornwallis	A British general	**General Cornwallis** surrendered to General Washington at the Battle of Yorktown.
Declaration of Independence	A statement explaining reasons for declaring independence	The **Declaration of Independence** announced the colonists' decision to separate from England and to create the United States.
Benjamin Franklin	A great printer and inventor	**Benjamin Franklin** went to France to get support for the colonists.
Fraunces Tavern	A meeting place in New York City	George Washington said goodbye to his troops at **Fraunces Tavern** at the end of the Revolutionary War.
Thomas Jefferson	A patriot from Virginia	**Thomas Jefferson** was asked to write the Declaration of Independence.
July 4, 1776	The day the Continental Congress approved the Declaration of Independence	Americans have celebrated Independence Day every year since the United States was born on **July 4, 1776**
King George	King of England during the Revolutionary War	**King George** refused to listen to the colonists.

52

TERM	DEFINITION	SENTENCE
General Lafayette	A French general	**General Lafayette** from France fought bravely of the side of the Americans.
Loyalists, or Tories	People who believed the colonies should belong to Britain	Some **loyalists** became spies for the British.
militia	An army composed of ordinary citizens	Farmers in the colonies joined the **militia** to defend their rights.
Minutemen	Men who could fight the British at a minute's notice	The **Minutemen** surprised the British and won the Battle of Concord.
Parliament	The British legislature	**Parliament** voted not to lift the tax on tea.
Patriots	Colonists against British rule	**Patriots** joined the militia to fight for freedom.
Quartering Act	A law passed by Britain	The **Quartering Act** forced the colonists in Boston to feed and house the British soldiers.
Red Coats	British soldiers	British soldiers wore bright **Red Coats** that were easy to see and made them easy targets.
Paul Revere	A Massachusetts patriot	**Paul Revere** sounded the alarm that the British were headed for Lexington.
"Shot heard round the world"	The beginning of the Revolutionary War	The Minutemen fired **"the shot heard round the world"** at the Battle of Concord where ordinary citizens defeated British troops.
Stamp Act	A tax on written and published material	The **Stamp Act**, a tax on all written material, made the colonists very angry.
Yorktown, Virginia	Where the last battle of the Revolution was fought	The Americans won the Revolutionary War at the Battle of **Yorktown**

53

Objective Questions

Circle the correct answer choice for each question.

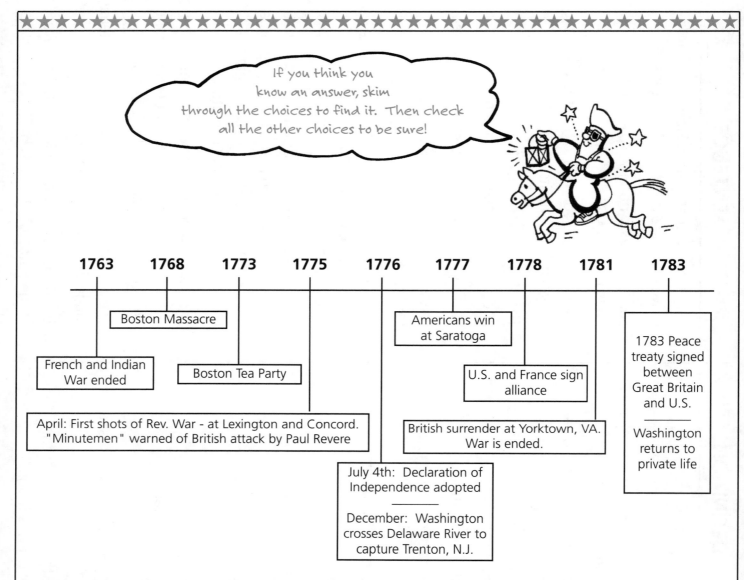

> If you think you know an answer, skim through the choices to find it. Then check all the other choices to be sure!

1763 1768 1773 1775 1776 1777 1778 1781 1783

Boston Massacre

French and Indian War ended

Boston Tea Party

April: First shots of Rev. War - at Lexington and Concord. "Minutemen" warned of British attack by Paul Revere

Americans win at Saratoga

U.S. and France sign alliance

British surrender at Yorktown, VA. War is ended.

July 4th: Declaration of Independence adopted
———
December: Washington crosses Delaware River to capture Trenton, N.J.

1783 Peace treaty signed between Great Britain and U.S.
———
Washington returns to private life

Base your answers to questions 1 through 6 on the timeline above.

1. When did the Revolutionary War begin?
a. 1768   b. 1775
c. 1776   d. 1777

2. How long did the fighting last?
a. 6 months   b. 8 years
c. 20 years   d. 6 years

3. In 1773 the colonists:
a. Threw English tea into Boston Harbor
b. Had a party with their English soldiers
c. Invaded Boston
d. Massacred the British

54

4. How many years are shown on this timeline?
a. 200
b. 30
c. 100
d. 20

5. About how old is the United States of America now?
a. About 400 years old
b. About 225 years old
c. About 200 years old
d. About 2000 years old

6. Why do we celebrate July 4th.?
a. It is the day we declared our independence from Great Britain
b. It is the day we won the Revolutionary War.
c. It is the day we adopted new states into our country.
d. It is the day we celebrate Thanksgiving.

---

7. What two nations fought in the French and Indian War?
a. The U.S. and France
b. The Indians and England
c. England and France
d. The Indians and France

8. France agreed to help the colonists right AFTER:
a. The colonists showed they could beat the British at Saratoga
b. The British surrendered at Yorktown
c. The French and Indian War
d. The Declaration of Independence was signed.

9. The words English and British refer to:
a. Two different people
b. The colonists and the people of England
c. The same people
d. The English Parliament and the Continental Congress

10. Paul Revere is famous for:
a. Serving with the Patriots
b. Warning of an attack
c. Winning the war
d. Firing the first shots of the War

Objective Questions

★★

11. Which of the following would NOT be an example of a primary source of information?

a. a letter written to King George

b. a letter from George Washington to his wife

c. a poem a colonial soldier wrote to his mother

d. an essay about 200 years of American history

Base your answers to numbers 12 and 13 on the picture below.

12. Which historic event is pictured here?

a. Paul Revere's warning

b. The battle at Yorktown

c. The French and Indian War

d. the Boston Tea Party

13. What does the crowd on the shore feel about this act?

a. They are surprised.

b. They are encouraging.

c. They are saddened.

d. They are confused.

14. What major principle did the Stamp Act violate?

a. No taxation without representation

b. Whatever is begun in anger, ends in shame.

c. A penny saved is a penny earned

d. Taxation often leads to inflation.

15. Who wrote the Declaration of Independence?

a. Thomas Jefferson

b. Benjamin Franklin

c. George Washington

d. Paul Revere

★★

Constructed-Response Questions

Write your answers to the questions in the spaces provided.

Constructed-response questions require good writing skills. Unlike multiple-choice questions, you must write the answer. Often more than one sentence is required for a complete response. (Many questions in this section require several sentences).

The Battle of Bunker Hill was fought on June 17, 1775. The well-trained British troops won, but only after the colonial militia ran out of ammunition.

1. Which side had an advantae in the fighting? Explain.

_____

_____

2. At the start of the battle, American Colonel William Prescott gave the following order: "Don't one of you fire until you see the whites of their eyes." Why do you think he said this? _____

_____

3. Who won the Battle of Bunker Hill? _____

Constructed-Response Questions

Below is an American cartoon showing the retreat of the British from Lexington, Massachusetts.

The British Soldiers, pictured with donkey heads, are
followed by the Colonial Minutemen.

4. Why do you think the artist gave the English soldiers donkey heads?

_____

_____

5. How do you think the colonists felt when they saw this cartoon?

_____

_____

_____

_____

Constructed-Response Questions

★★

Patrick Henry was a great orator (speaker). Here is pat of a famous speech he gave to the Virginia Assembly on March 23, 1775.

...The war is inevitable--and let it come! I repeat, sir, let it come! ..Is life so dear, or peace so sweet, as to be purchased at the price of chains and slavery? Forbid it, Almighty God! I know not what course other may take; but as for me, give me liberty or give me death!

6. How does Patrick Henry feel about fighting a war with England?

_____

_____

_____

7. What does he say life is like under British rule?

_____

_____

_____

8. What price is he willing to pay for his freedom from Great Britain?

_____

_____

_____

59

★★

Constructed-Response Questions

**This drawing appeared in the _Boston Gazette_ on May 21, 1754.
Base your answers to questions 9 through 12 on it.**

9. What does each piece of he snake represent?

   _____

   _____

10. What is the snake telling the colonies to do?

   _____

   _____

11. Which group of colonists would favor this message, the Loyalists
    or the Patriots? Why?

   _____

   _____

12. What does the picture suggest will happen if the colonists do not join together?

   _____

   _____

   _____

OUR GOVERNMENT: Checks And Balances

After surveying the story, I can tell that:

1. The state's equivalent to the President is _____.
   a. the mayor   b. the governor

2. The document that begins with the words "We the People. . ." is
   _____.
   a. the Declaration of Independence   b.   the Constitution

3. The justices of the Supreme Court serve for _____.
   a. six years   b. life

After looking at the objective questions and constructed-response questions, I can tell that:

4. The picture on the Great Seal of the U.S. shows _____.
   a. an eagle   b. the capitol building

5. Only the _____ can print money.
   a. states   b. federal government

ANSWER BOX
1. The state's equivalent to the President is the governor.
2. The document that begins with the words "We the People..." is the constitution.
3. The justices of the Supreme Court serve for life.
4. The picture on the Great Seal of the U.S. shows an eagle.
5. Only the federal government can print money.

Read the following selection carefully. Stop after each section to retell the main idea in your own words.

★★

The Revolutionary War was won. The thirteen colonies became the thirteen states. Each state had its own government.   Before the war had ended, the Continental Congress wrote **the Articles of Confederation.** These rules were supposed to join the states together. It did not work. Each state acted alone, doing what was best for itself.

The thirteen states needed to work together. The Founding Fathers called a **Constitutional Convention**. This meeting of state delegates chose men to write a new document. In order to act together, the states needed a strong central government. This is called the **federal government**. The delegate also wanted to be sure that the government would be run by the people who live in the country. This is called a **democracy**.

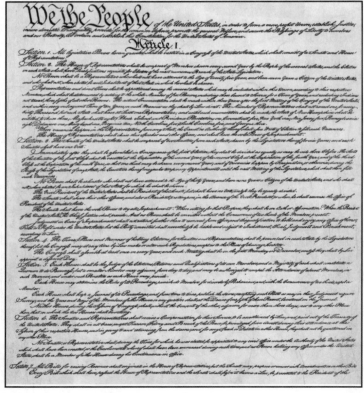

U.S. Constitution

THE CONSTITUTION

The final document, ***The Constitution***, created **three branches of government**. This *Separation of Powers* makes it impossible for one man or one group to take over the country. More than 200 years later, this is still the law of our land.

The three branches are the **Executive Branch**, **the Legislative Branch**, and the **Judicial Branch**. Each branch has its own special job. The key to the success of this system is that they also work together. The **Founding Fathers** called this **Checks and Balances**. Each branch is controlled by the other two branches.

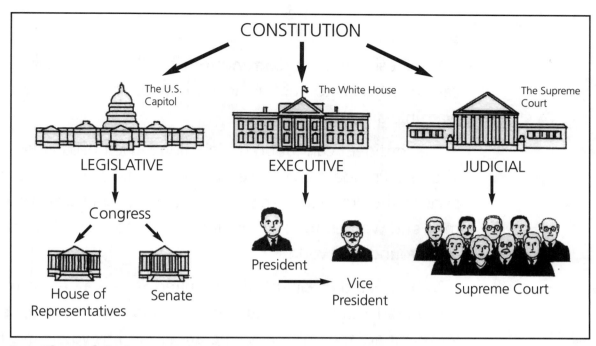

CONSTITUTION

The U.S. Capitol   The White House   The Supreme Court

LEGISLATIVE   EXECUTIVE   JUDICIAL

Congress

House of Representatives   Senate

President   Vice President   Supreme Court

Branches of Government

THE EXECUTIVE BRANCH

The President of the United States is the head of the Executive Branch. The duty of the President is to be sure federal laws are obeyed. He is the most important person in the Executive Branch. Congress sends the President **bills** it has voted on. If he approves of a bill, he signs it. Then it becomes a law. If he is against the bill, he **vetoes** it. A veto from the President makes it almost certain that a bill will not become a law.

If **Congress** still wants a bill to pass, however, it takes another vote. If two-thirds of the Senate and the House of Representatives vote yes, the Congress **overrides** the President's veto. The bill becomes a law. This is checks and balances in action.

The President picks the judges of the Supreme Court. But Congress has to approve his choices. In this way, Congress checks both the President and the Supreme Court.

As the American Head of State, the President may make **treaties** with other countries. Here again, there is a check. The Senate must approve, or there will be no treaty.

63

The President is the **Commander-in-Chief** of the Armed Forces. He can send troops to fight against other countries. But he cannot declare war unless Congress agrees.

The President cannot do his job alone. He needs aides and advisers. The Vice President is his chief adviser. He takes over if something happens to the President. The President also has a **Cabinet**. He chooses men and women to keep him informed about activities in the country and around the world.

To be elected President of the United States, a person must be born in the United States and be at least 35 years old. The President and Vice President are the only ones who are elected by voters in *all* states. They are elected for a term of four years. The President and Vice President may be re-elected. They may serve for only two terms, or eight years. During his term of office, the President lives at the White House in **Washington, D.C.** His offices are there, too.

THE LEGISLATIVE BRANCH

The Legislative Branch is Congress. Congress makes laws to control trade between the states and between the United States and other countries. It soon becomes clear why this is so necessary. What if each state made its own agreements with other countries? What if each state had a different kind of money? Life in the United States would be very confusing! That is why having a strong federal government was such a good idea. Congress, alone, has the right to declare war.

Some states are large and have many people. Other states have smaller populations. The men at the Constitutional Convention argued about how many representatives in Congress each state should have. Some thought all the states should have the same number no matter what their size. Others wanted to base the number of representatives on the number of people living in each state. A legislature with two parts was a very clever way to give equal representation to everyone. This is how it works.

THE HOUSE OF REPRESENTATIVES

A state is divided into areas, called congressional districts. Each district elects a person to represent it in the **House of Representatives**. So the states with the highest population have the most representatives. Elections for the House of Representatives are held every two years. A representative may serve as many times as the people wish to elect him or her.

The House of Representatives

New Hampshire = 2 Representatives

Louisiana = 7 Representatives

THE SENATE

There are several differences between the House and the Senate. The most important one is that in the **Senate** every state is represented by two senators. In this way, all states, large and small, are equally represented. Senators serve for six years at a time. Like the representatives, senators may be re-elected over and over again.

Both the Senate and the House of Representatives must vote and approve a bill before it can be sent to the President to be signed. Only then can it become a law.

The Senate

Current Supreme Court: It's nine members are appointed and serve for life.

THE JUDICIAL BRANCH

The Judicial Branch of the government is made up of the courts. The United States **Supreme Court** is the highest court in the land. This court is made up of nine justices who are appointed by the President. Because they serve for life, new justices are chosen only when one of them dies or retires.

The Supreme Court hears cases about the meaning of certain laws. It checks to see if a case is constitutional: Does it follow the rules laid out in the Constitution?

When the Supreme Court makes a decision, it is very difficult to change it. This can be done only through an **amendment**, or change, to the Constitution. This is a long and serious process.

STATE GOVERNMENTS

The Founding Fathers gave the states the right to control things within their borders. So each state has a state government very much like the federal system. The executive branch is made up of the **governor** and his or her advisers. The governor makes sure the laws of the state are carried out. The legislative branch is called the state legislature. It makes the laws for that state. The judicial branch is made up of state courts. They make sure the laws passed by that state are fair. The state governments work on a system of checks and balances just like the national government.

CHECKS AND BALANCES

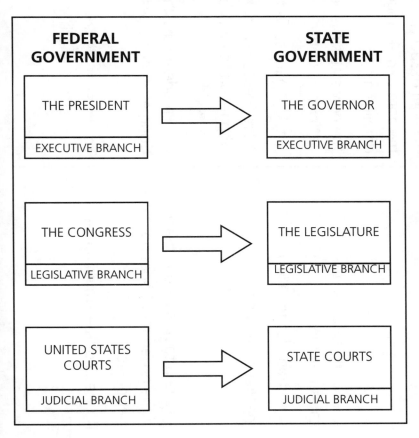

FEDERAL GOVERNMENT	STATE GOVERNMENT
THE PRESIDENT EXECUTIVE BRANCH	THE GOVERNOR EXECUTIVE BRANCH
THE CONGRESS LEGISLATIVE BRANCH	THE LEGISLATURE LEGISLATIVE BRANCH
UNITED STATES COURTS JUDICIAL BRANCH	STATE COURTS JUDICIAL BRANCH

For more than 200 years, this system of checks and balances has been successful. Each of the branches of government has the power to affect the other branches. The Executive Branch carries out the laws; the Legislative Branch makes the laws; the Judicial Branch makes sure the laws follow the Constitution.

Our Federal and State Governments: Parallel Structures

Name the three branches of government.

Who is a member of each branch?

What job does each branch do?

What does "Checks and Balances" mean?

TERMS TO REMEMBER The following Names, Dates, Places, and Words about Our Government are important to remember. Study them carefully. The sentences will help you understand their meanings.

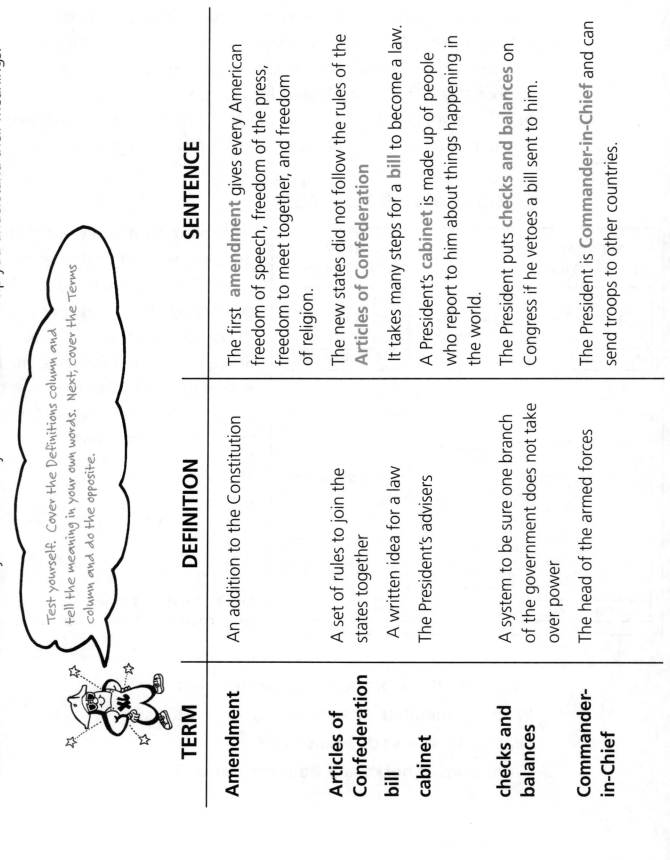

Test yourself. Cover the Definitions column and tell the meaning in your own words. Next, cover the Terms column and do the opposite.

TERM	DEFINITION	SENTENCE
Amendment	An addition to the Constitution	The first **amendment** gives every American freedom of speech, freedom of the press, freedom to meet together, and freedom of religion.
Articles of Confederation	A set of rules to join the states together	The new states did not follow the rules of the **Articles of Confederation**
bill	A written idea for a law	It takes many steps for a **bill** to become a law.
cabinet	The President's advisers	A President's **cabinet** is made up of people who report to him about things happening in the world.
checks and balances	A system to be sure one branch of the government does not take over power	The President puts **checks and balances** on Congress if he vetoes a bill sent to him.
Commander-in-Chief	The head of the armed forces	The President is **Commander-in-Chief** and can send troops to other countries.

TERM	DEFINITION	SENTENCE
Congress	The legislature	Congress is made up of two parts, the Senate and the House of Representatives.
Constitution	A plan of government	A constitution explains how the government is set up.
Constitutional Convention	A meeting of delegates from every state to choose men to write the Constitution	The Constitutional Convention appointed 14 members to write the Constitution.
Democracy	A government run by the people, for the people	In a democracy citizens elect representatives who pass laws for the good of all.
Executive Branch	Carries out laws	The president of the United States is the head of the Executive Branch
Federal Government	A system that gives power to state and central governments	A federal government is a union of states with the power divided between the states and the central government.
Founding Fathers	Members of the Constitutional Convention	The Founding Fathers met at the Constitutional Convention to outline the form of the new government.
governor	Head of a state government	The governor is part of the executive branch and carries out the laws of his or her state.
House of Representatives, or "The House"	A part of congress	The number of representatives a state sends to the House of Representatives depends on how many people live in that state.
Judicial Branch	The court system	The Supreme Court, the highest court in the land, decides whether new laws are constitutional.

TERM	DEFINITION	SENTENCE
Legislative Branch	The law making body	The **legislative branch**, or Congress, makes laws.
override a veto	Vote to allow a bill to pass that the President does not want	Congress may **override a veto** by taking a vote to pass it, after the President has vetoed it.
Senate	a part of Congress	The **Senate** and the House of Representatives together make the laws for our country.
Supreme Court	the highest court in the United States	The **Supreme Court** is the final authority for any questions about the Constitution.
Three Branches of Government	the Executive, the Legislative, and the Judicial branches	**The three branches of government** share the power to govern.
treaty	an agreement between two countries	Only the federal government can make a **treaty** with a foreign country.
veto	the right of the President to refuse to sign a bill into law	When the President **vetoes** a bill, it can still become a law if two-thirds of the members of Congress approve it.
Washington, D.C.	the capital city of the United States of America	The three branches of our government meet in **Washington**, D.C.

Objective Questions

Circle the correct answer choice for each question.

Be careful of words such as BUT, NOT, EXCEPT. They indicate a change in the question asked. They are often written in capitals to warn the test taker.

1. What is the main reason that there are three parts to our government?

a. There is a lot of work to do.

b. It prevents one part from having all the power.

c. There are three parts of our country to govern.

d. The President's Cabinet has three members.

2. Small states like Delaware and large states like California have all the following in common, EXCEPT:

a. they both vote for the President and Vice-President

b. they both send two Senators to the Senate

c. they both send 10 representatives to the House

d. they both must obey the Constitution of the United States

3. Which group of words best defines a veto?

a. Congress does not approve a bill.

b. The President refuses to sign a bill.

c. The Supreme Court says a law goes against the Constitution.

d. Only the Senate approves a bill.

★★

Use the Venn Diagram, below, to answer questions 4 through 7.

DUTIES OF THE FEDERAL AND STATE GOVERNMENTS

ONLY the Federal Government   **Both**   **ONLY the State Government**

Controls foreign trade
and trade between states

Delivers the mail

Prints money

Settles quarrels
between states

Can Declare war

Collect taxes

Borrow money

Enforce the law &
punish those that
break laws

Make laws

Controls trade within state

Runs public schools

Commands National Guard

Decides who can vote in
state & local elections

4. According to the Venn diagram, BOTH the state and federal governments
    can:
    a. print money   b. borrow money
    c. run public schools   d. run the post office

5. Only the federal government can:
    a. make trade deals with England
    b. collect taxes
    c. make laws
    d. make large trade deals within a state

6. Only the state government can:
    a. run public schools   b. make laws
    c. run the post office   d. control trade

★★

Objective Questions

★★★

7. Which statement below seems to be true?
   a. The federal government deals with war and money while the state government controls schools and taxes.
   b. The federal government deals with issues between states while the state government controls affairs within its borders.
   c. The federal government deals with public issues while the state government deals with private issues.
   d. The federal government deals with large corporations and foreign governments while the state government is responsible for passing laws and collecting taxes.

_____

8. The governor of a state is elected by:
   a. the voters of that state
   b. the voters of the country
   c. the voters in the capital city
   d. the voters in the state legislature

9. All of the following are components of our government EXCEPT:
   a. The President appoints Supreme Court justices.
   b. The President appoints Senators.
   c. Members of Congress have limited terms of office.
   d. The President must be born in the United States.

10. The terms "federal" and "national" refer to:
   a. our central government
   b. our central and state governments
   c. the city and town governments
   d. our system of checks and balances

11. The U.S. President:
   a. has more power than the Congress.
   b. is the highest ranking member of the army, navy and air force.
   c. can declare war against our enemies.
   d. may serve as many terms as the people choose to elect him /her

12. Which term best defines a government in which the people are the most important part of the government?
   a. capitalism
   b. democracy
   c. dictatorship
   d. monarchy

Base your answers to questions 13 through 15 on the three pictures below.

White House

U.S. Capitol

U.S. Supreme Court

13. Which is the only building where the members are appointed, not elected?
   a. U.S. Capitol   b. White House
   c. U.S. Supreme Court   d. None of the above

14. Where do the House of Representatives and the Senate meet?
   a. U.S. Capitol   b. White House
   c. U.S. Supreme Court   e. The Capitol and the Supreme Court

15. In which building does the Commander in Chief of the Armed forces live?
   a. U.S. Capitol   b. White House
   c. U.S. Supreme Court   d. The Senate

Constructed-Response Questions

Write your answers to the questions that follow in the spaces provided.

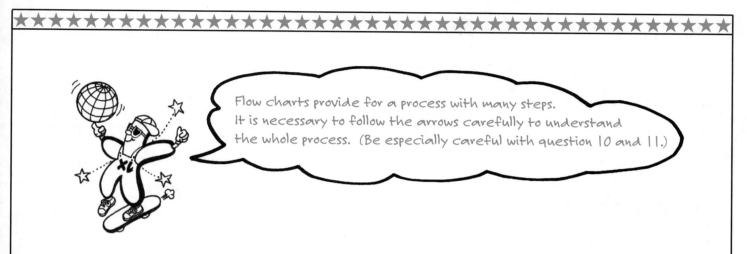

Flow charts provide for a process with many steps. It is necessary to follow the arrows carefully to understand the whole process. (Be especially careful with question 10 and 11.)

The chart below shows each state in the Union and how it ranked in population compared to the others. Use this information and your knowledge of government to answer questions 1 through 4.

Population Rank in 1790
(number 1 represents highest population)

Connecticut	8
Delaware	16
Georgia	13
Kentucky	14
Maine	11
Maryland	6
Massachusetts	4
New Hampshire	10
New Jersey	9
New York	5
North Carolina	3
Pennsylvania	2
Rhode Island	15
South Carolina	7
Tennessee	17
Vermont	12
Virginia	1

Constructed-Response Questions

1. How many states were part of our country in 1790?

_____

_____

_____

_____

2. What state had the most people living there?

_____

_____

_____

_____

3. What state would have the fewest members in the House of Representatives?

_____

_____

_____

_____

4. Based on your knowledge of our government, how many members did New Hampshire elect to the Senate?

_____

_____

_____

_____

Constructed-Response Questions

Study the symbols on the Great Seal of the United States. Base your answers to questions 5 through 7 on this document.

Crest with 13 stars

Eagle: Our National Bird

Olive branch: Stands for peace

Shield in red, white, and blue stands for our Congress

Motto: Means "many states unite in one government". Our motto is "E Pluribus Unum."

Arrows: Mean that our country will fight back if attacked

THE GREAT SEAL OF THE UNITED STATES

5. The Bald Eagle holds both the olive branch and arrows. What message does this send?

_____

_____

6. Name the symbols that contain 13 objects. Why was the number 13 chosen?

_____

_____

Constructed-Response Questions

★★★

7. Why do you think this motto is a good description of America?

_____

_____

Base your answers to questions 8 through 12 on the flow chart located in the following page.

8. How do you think a member of the House or Senate decides what bill to introduce?

_____

_____

9. Why is it wise for a committee to discuss and approve a bill before it comes before the whole House or Senate?

_____

_____

10. Explain how a bill can become a law even if the President does not sign it.

_____

_____

11. Bills can be introduced in either the House or Senate. Explain what would be different in this flow chart if the bill were introduced in the Senate instead of the House.

_____

_____

12. How does this flow chart show Checks and Balances?

_____

_____

★★★

Constructed-Response Questions

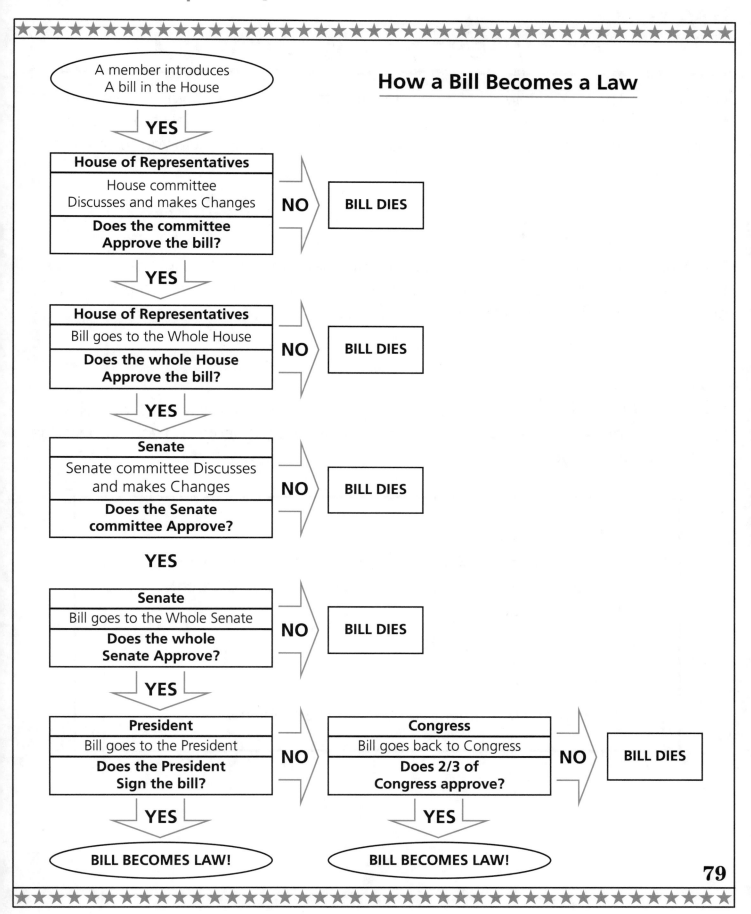

How a Bill Becomes a Law

A member introduces
A bill in the House

YES

House of Representatives

House committee
Discusses and makes Changes

**Does the committee
Approve the bill?**

NO → **BILL DIES**

YES

House of Representatives

Bill goes to the Whole House

**Does the whole House
Approve the bill?**

NO → **BILL DIES**

YES

Senate

Senate committee Discusses
and makes Changes

**Does the Senate
committee Approve?**

NO → **BILL DIES**

YES

Senate

Bill goes to the Whole Senate

**Does the whole
Senate Approve?**

NO → **BILL DIES**

YES

President

Bill goes to the President

**Does the President
Sign the bill?**

NO →

Congress

Bill goes back to Congress

**Does 2/3 of
Congress approve?**

NO → **BILL DIES**

YES

BILL BECOMES LAW!

YES

BILL BECOMES LAW!

DBQ II

DOCUMENT-BASED QUESTION

Directions: The task below is based on documents 1 through 5. It will test your ability to work with historical documents as well as your knowledge of social studies. Study each document, and answer the questions that follow. They will help you to organize your essay.

Historical Background:

The American colonists rebelled against the unfair laws of Great Britain, the government that ruled them. After winning their independence, they set up their own government, one that would represent <u>all</u> the people of the country.

Task:

Part A is made up of short-answer questions. After reading the essay question below, answer each question fully. Use the information in the documents and your knowledge of social studies for your answers.

> ## Essay Question:
>
> Explain the problems the American Colonists had with Great Britain and how they made sure their new government would be different. In your essay be sure to include:
>
> • What the Americans wanted
>
> • What they did about it
>
> • How their new government corrected these problems.

Document-Based Question

Part A—Short-Answer Questions

Directions: Study each document and answer the questions that follow. Base your answers on the documents provided as well as your knowledge of social studies.

DOCUMENT 1

Samuel Adams, a famous patriot, spoke out about the taxes Great Britain had put on the colonists. Here is part of what he said:

> ". . . if our trade may be taxed, why not our lands? Why not the crops of our lands and everything we own? This destroys our charter right to govern and tax ourselves. If taxes are put upon us without our having a representative present, are we not changed from a free people to miserable slaves?" (Simplified)

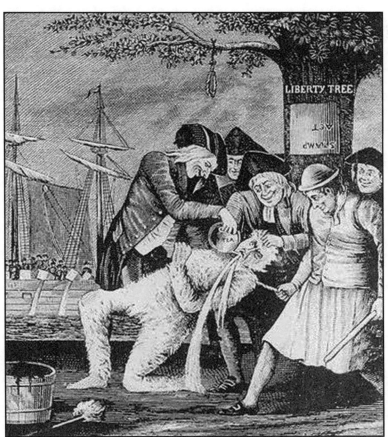

This print shows Bostonians tarring and feathering a tax collector and forcing tea down his throat. In the background, men throw tea from a ship in the harbor.

Study both Samuel Adams' words and the picture above. Then answer the following questions.

Document-Based Question

★★★

1. If the colonists accepted England's new taxes, what did Adams think would follow?

_____

_____

_____

_____

_____

_____

_____

2. What did Samuel Adams object to more than taxes themselves?

_____

_____

_____

_____

_____

_____

_____

_____

_____

_____

3. Which tax are the colonists against in the picture on the previous page?

_____

_____

_____

★★★

Document-Based Question

DOCUMENT 2

Ralph Waldo Emerson wrote a poem about the Battle of Lexington and Concord. It begins with:

"By the rude bridge that arched the flood
Their flag to April's bridge unfurled,
Here once the embattled farmers stood
And fired the 'shot heard around the world.'"

Minuteman Statue, Lexington, Massachusetts

1. What was the Minuteman's job before the Revolutionary War?

_____

_____

_____

_____

_____

2. Why were they called Minutemen?

_____

_____

_____

_____

_____

3. What does the "shot heard around the world" mean?

_____

_____

_____

Document-Based Question

The Battle of Yorktown

The Battle of Yorktown, 1781

The Battle of Yorktown, in Virginia, was the last battle of the Revolutionary War. From the map above and your knowledge of the Revolutionary War, answer the following questions.

1. Where are the French and American armies?

_____

_____

2. The British camps are on the river. Why can't they escape out to sea by water?

_____

_____

3. What happened after the British lost this battle?

_____

_____

_____

Document-Based Question

★★

DOCUMENT 4

OUR FEDERAL GOVERNMENT
A System of Checks and Balances

EXECUTIVE BRANCH

President

Vice-President

Cabinet

Job: Approve (or veto) the laws

JUDICIAL BRANCH

Supreme Court
(9 Justices)

Lower courts

Job: Decide if laws agree with the constitution

LEGISLATIVE BRANCH

House of Representatives	Senate
435 Representatives	100 Senators
(Number from each state based on its population)	(2 from each state)

Job: Make the laws

Base your answers to the questions below on the diagram as well as your knowledge of how our government works.

1. How do all three branches of government share the job of making laws for our country?

_____

_____

2. How does the Constitution make sure that people from all states, big and small, have a part in making the laws that govern them?

_____

_____

3. Why didn't the writers of the Constitution plan for a king?

_____

★★

Document-Based Question

DOCUMENT 5

The Bill of Rights is a list of 10 amendments, or changes, to the Constitution. They guarantee the rights of the people. The following is an explanation of Amendments 1-6.

Base your answers to the questions that follow on this document.

**The Bill of Rights
Articles 1-6**

Amendment 1: States that people can speak or write their opinions. They can follow any religion they wish. They can hold peaceful meetings and ask the government to correct things they think are unfair.

Amendment 2: States that the government cannot stop people from owning weapons.

Amendment 3: States that people cannot be forced to have soldiers stay in their houses.

Amendment 4: States that people cannot be searched or arrested, or have their houses searched without good reason.

Amendment 5: States that a person cannot be forced to say anything that may help to convict him. If he is found not guilty, he cannot be put on trial for the same crime again.

Amendment 6: States that if a person is accused of a crime, he or she has the right to a speedy trial by a jury and has the right to a lawyer.

The colonists had many complaints against Great Britain. Which amendment, above, corrects each of these problems?

a. King George forced colonists to have British soldiers stay in their houses. _____

b. Colonists who wrote articles about unfair British laws were arrested. _____

c. Those who spoke out against the King were arrested. _____

d. Governors were allowed to search the colonists' homes whenever they wished. _____

e. The colonists did not have a right to a trial by a jury. _____

86

★★

Document-Based Question

★★

Directions: Review the documents in Part A and your answers. They will help you to write the essay below.

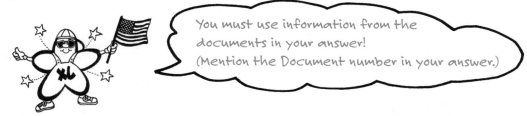

You must use information from the documents in your answer!
(Mention the Document number in your answer.)

Historical Background:

The American colonists rebelled against the unfair laws of Great Britain, the government that ruled them. After winning their independence, they set up their own government, one that would represent all the people of the country.

Task:

Use the documents in Part A, your answers, and your knowledge of social studies to write the essay below.

Essay Question:

Explain the problems the American Colonists had with Great Britain and how they made sure their new government would be different. In your essay be sure to include:

- What the Americans wanted

- What they did about it

- How their new government corrected these problems.

Use the graphic organizer on the next page to organize your answer!

87

★★

GRAPHIC ORGANIZER

Take notes. Do not use full sentences.

What Americans Wanted		What they did about it		How new government corrected problem	
Doc.	Notes	Doc.	Notes	Doc.	Notes
1	Right to decide own taxes (with representation in legislature)				
1	Right to govern selves				
5	Right to speak out against King or government leaders				
5	_____				
5	_____				
5	_____				
5	_____				

Student Response

Use the information in your graphic organizer to write a detailed essay.

Look at DBQ I and the Editor's Page for help in organizing this paper!

Document-Based Question

Go to the Editor's Page ➡

UNIT 5: The Story of
THE INDUSTRIAL REVOLUTION

After surveying the story, I can tell that:

1. The *Clermont* was the first _____.
   a. steamboat
   b. barge

2. The Erie Canal brought more _____ to our country.
   a. trade and shipping
   b. pollution and disease

3. The telephone was invented by _____.
   a. Samuel Morse
   b. Alexander Graham Bell

After looking at the objective questions and constructed-response questions, I can tell that:

4. The Erie Canal is located in _____.
   a. New York State
   b. Massachusetts

5. Tom Thumb, a steam locomotive, was invented by _____.
   a. Peter Cooper
   b. Benjamin Franklin

ANSWER BOX

1. The *Clermont* was the first steamboat.
2. The Erie Canal brought more trade and shipping to our country.
3. The telephone was invented by Alexander Graham Bell.
4. The Erie Canal is located in New York State.
5. Tom Thumb, a steam locomotive, was invented by Peter Cooper.

Read the following selection carefully. Stop after each section to retell the main idea in your own words.

91

The Story of The Industrial Revolution

★★★

A **revolution** is a time of sudden change. Sometimes a revolution is a war. The United States won its independence by fighting the Revolutionary War in 1776. Not long after, the Industrial Revolution took place. This peaceful revolution changed how people worked, traveled, and lived. At this time, many talented people invented new machines. This led to an exciting era that would change America.

Fulton and the Steam Engine

Fulton's boat, The Clermont

The invention of the steam engine changed **transportation**. Steam ships replaced sailing ships. The new ships carried people and cargo across the ocean faster and cheaper than before. This meant that many more people could come across the ocean to find jobs and new lives here.

Robert Fulton learned about the steam engine when he was in England. He was sure this engine could drive a ship. Back in the United States, he designed a ship with a flat bottom. A paddle wheel hung on the middle of each side. Then he put a steam engine in front of the wheels.

The ship looked strange to people because of its puffing smoke stacks. Some people laughed at it and called it "Fulton's Folly." Fulton named the boat, the *Clermont*. On August 17, 1807, the ship made its first trip from New York City to Albany in 32 hours. This was much faster than before. Fulton said, "The power of propelling boats by steam is now fully proved." The $7 trip was cheap and popular.

The Erie Canal

At just about the same time, Americans were on the move, too. Businessmen in the East wanted to sell their goods to customers west of New York. The **Appalachian Mountains** stood in the way. Traders wanted to get their goods from New York to Buffalo, a city on Lake Erie. Lake Erie flowed into the other **Great Lakes** and into many rivers. But people could ship their goods only as far as Albany. Three hundred miles of poor roads lay between Albany and Buffalo. A water route from Albany to Buffalo would mean a boat could go from New York City all the way to the Midwest. (See map on page 100.)

The Erie Canal encouraged trading and shipping. Mules walking on paths along side pulled the barges.

DeWitt Clinton became governor of New York State. He was sure there was a way to connect the **Hudson River** with the Great Lakes. The answer was a manmade waterway, a canal. In 1817, work began on the **Erie Canal**. A great ditch, deep enough for a boat, needed to be dug. Some people thought it couldn't be done and called it *DeWitt's Ditch*. It would cost too much money, over 7 million dollars.

Work went ahead anyway. By 1825, the Erie Canal cut across New York State. Ships traveled from New York City up the Hudson to Albany. Then they crossed the Erie Canal to Buffalo. This made New York America's largest port. Of course, the ships returned by the same route. Before the canal, a ton of cargo took at least three weeks to get from Lake Erie to New York City. It cost $100. That same ton of cargo made the trip in seven days at a cost of $10 using the Erie Canal. The Erie

Canal was good for New York. It brought people and business to the whole state. Cities and towns sprang up along the canal.

The Erie Canal was good for the rest of the country, too. People crowded onto steamboats. They headed west to build cities and to develop farms. Immigrants from other countries joined them. There was room for everyone.

Paying for the canal was not a problem. New York State charged ships a **toll** each time they passed through. The canal was paid for in less than ten years. The steam engine was once called Fulton's Folly. The manmade canal, was once called DeWitt's Ditch. In the end, the two changed the face of this nation.

Cross Country on the Railroad

Tom Thumb, the first locomotive powered by steam

Peter Cooper

Our nation is 3,000 miles wide. The country needed fast transportation by land, too. Once again, steam played an important part. The Baltimore and Ohio Railroad began operation in 1828 with horse-drawn cars. But in 1830, **Peter Cooper** invented *Tom Thumb*. This was a locomotive powered by steam. It improved travel on land. Trains could carry people and cargo great distances. Soon, railroad tracks crossed the nation. As a result there was no stopping the United States. Transportation flowed freely across our great land.

Edison and Electric Light

Edison's invention of the light bulb changed the world.

Another invention caused a revolution in the use of **energy**. People had been reading by candlelight or kerosene lamplight. **Thomas Alva Edison** changed the world when he invented the light bulb. He designed a way to bring light and power to a large area.

One dark night, in 1882, Edison flipped a switch. Right away electric lights shone from 40 buildings in New York City. Edison once said, "I would like to live about 300 years. I think I have IDEAS enough to keep me busy that long." In a way his wish came true. People are still inventing things based on Edison's ideas.

Morse Invents the Telegraph

Samuel Morse also worked with electricity. He thought it could be used for **communication**. He invented a code that could send messages along an electric wire. Morse asked Congress to give him money to "wire America." He then strung a wire between Baltimore and Washington, D.C. He sent a message. It worked! By 1840, telegraph wires reached from coast to coast.

A replica of Bell's first telephone

Bell Invents the Telephone

Alexander Graham Bell found a way to send the sound of the human voice across wires. In 1876, he invented the telephone. The first telephone call was placed between two towns that were eight miles apart. Soon, poles and wires lined up across the country. The Bell Telephone Company made it possible for everyone to use a phone.

This made huge changes in people's lives. It allowed them to do business faster. Friends and families could talk to persons in other parts of the country.

The Industrial Revolution included these inventions in transportation, energy, and communication. They helped America grow rich and strong.

R E C I T E

Name one famous invention of the Industrial Revolution in transportation, energy, and communication.

Identify the inventor of each.

TERMS TO REMEMBER   The following Names, Dates, Places, and Words about The Industrial Revolution are important to remember. Study them carefully. The sentences will help you understand their meanings.

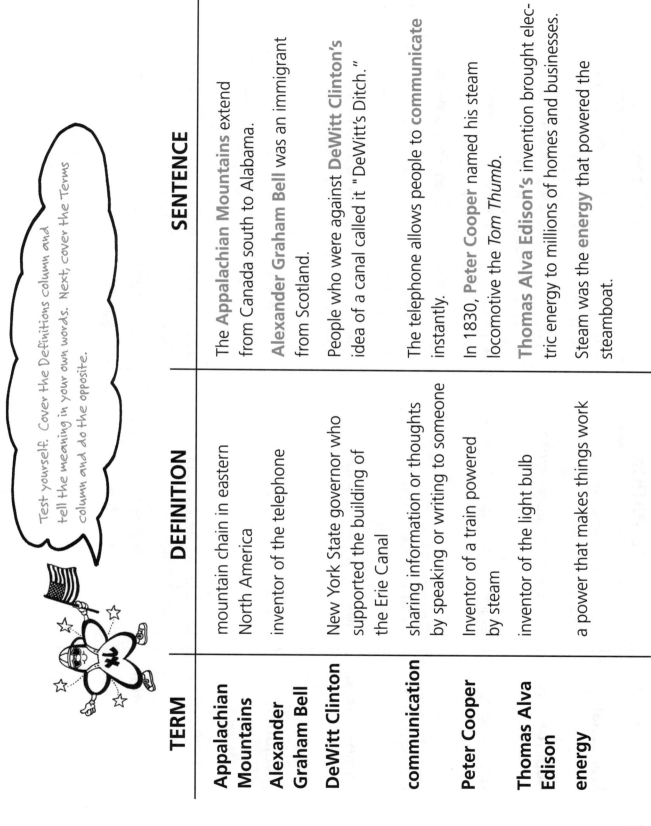

Test yourself. Cover the Definitions column and tell the meaning in your own words. Next, cover the Terms column and do the opposite.

TERM	DEFINITION	SENTENCE
Appalachian Mountains	mountain chain in eastern North America	The **Appalachian Mountains** extend from Canada south to Alabama.
Alexander Graham Bell	inventor of the telephone	**Alexander Graham Bell** was an immigrant from Scotland.
DeWitt Clinton	New York State governor who supported the building of the Erie Canal	People who were against **DeWitt Clinton's** idea of a canal called it "DeWitt's Ditch."
communication	sharing information or thoughts by speaking or writing to someone	The telephone allows people to **communicate** instantly.
Peter Cooper	Inventor of a train powered by steam	In 1830, **Peter Cooper** named his steam locomotive the *Tom Thumb.*
Thomas Alva Edison	inventor of the light bulb	**Thomas Alva Edison's** invention brought electric energy to millions of homes and businesses.
energy	a power that makes things work	Steam was the **energy** that powered the steamboat.

TERM	DEFINITION	SENTENCE
Erie Canal	A manmade waterway in New York State	The Erie Canal stretches all the way from Albany to Buffalo in New York State.
Robert Fulton	inventor of the steam engine	In 1807, Robert Fulton's steamboat, the Clermont, made its first trip.
Great Lakes	largest lakes in North America	A good way to remember the names of the five Great Lakes is to remember HOMES: Huron, Ontario, Michigan, Erie, Superior.
Hudson River	important river in eastern New York State	The Hudson River flows into the Atlantic Ocean at New York City.
Samuel Morse	inventor of the telegraph	The Morse Code, a way to send messages using dots and dashes, was named after Samuel Morse
revolution	a great and sudden change	The Industrial Revolution was a time when people began to use machines to make or move things.
toll	fee paid to travel on a bridge, road, or waterway	To pay for the Erie Canal, a toll was charged for all boats using it.
transportation	moving people or things from one place to another	The railroad is a cheap and easy means of transportation

Objective Questions

Circle the correct answer choice for each question below.

Read all answer choices. Often choice "a" may seem like the correct answer, but "d" is even better.

1. Which of the following was NOT a part of the Industrial Revolution?

a. The steamboat
c. the Revolutionary War
b. The Erie Canal
d. the light bulb

2. One result of the Industrial Revolution was:

a. people emigrated to Europe.
b. U.S. industry grew.
c. Thomas Edison was born.
d. a new government was formed.

3. The Erie Canal served to:

a. make the West a crowded place.
b. connect the Hudson River to the Atlantic Ocean.
c. place New York State into long-term debt.
d. make transportation cheaper and faster.

★★★

Base your answers to questions 4 through 5 on the map below.

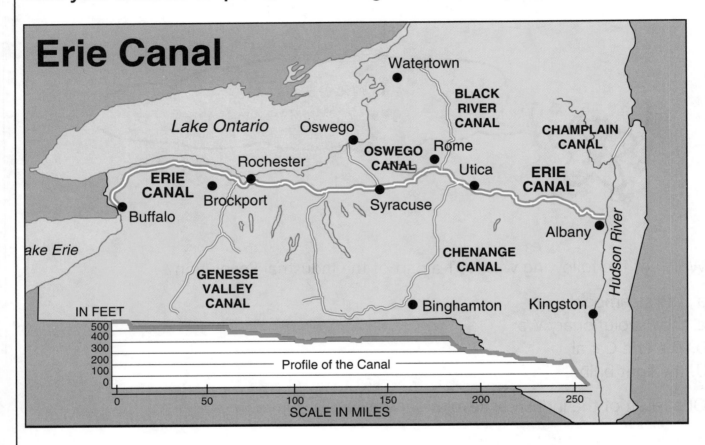

4. Which cities on the Erie Canal are farthest apart?

a. Rochester and Buffalo

b. Albany and Buffalo

c. Syracuse and Albany

d. Buffalo and Kingston

5. At which three cities would a ship stop along the Erie Canal?

a. Utica, Syracuse, and Rochester

b. Albany, Rome, and Binghamton

c. Kingston, Albany, and Utica

d. Buffalo, Brockport, and Oswego

★★★

6. What do Samuel Morse and Alexander Graham Bell have in common?
a. They invented a means of communication.
b. They invented a means of transportation.
c. They made travel cheaper.
d. They were writers

7. The Appalachians are:
a. a cross-country railroad
b. a mountain range
c. a canal
d. an invention

8. All of the following led to more efficient transportation in the U.S. EXCEPT:
a. the telephone
b. the Erie Canal
c. the railroad
d. the steam engine

9. The Industrial Revolution is an example of a:
a. peaceful change
b. war
c. treaty
d. document

10. Robert Fulton and DeWitt Clinton can both be described as:
a. men who were scientists
b. men who ran for office
c. men who were foolish
d. men who believed in their ideas

11. All of the following run on electric energy EXCEPT:
a. the steamboat
b. the telephone
c. the telegraph
d. the light bulb

Objective Questions

★★

Base your answers to questions 12 through 15 on the Time Line below.

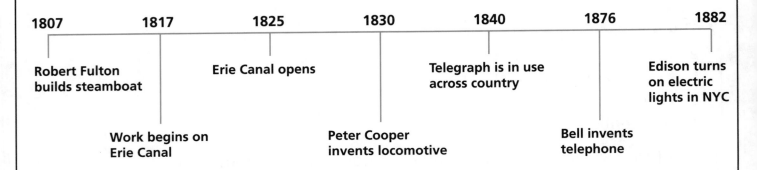

Technology Timeline

| 1807 | 1817 | 1825 | 1830 | 1840 | 1876 | 1882 |

Robert Fulton builds steamboat

Erie Canal opens

Telegraph is in use across country

Edison turns on electric lights in NYC

Work begins on Erie Canal

Peter Cooper invents locomotive

Bell invents telephone

12. Which of the following events happened first?
   a. The Erie Canal opened.
   b. Bell invented the telephone.
   c. The steam locomotive was invented.
   d. Robert Fulton built the steamboat.

13. How many years are shown on this time line?
   a. 82   b. 75
   c. 40   d. 80

14. The Erie Canal was built between:
   a. 1807 and 1825
   b. 1817 and 1825
   c. 1817 and 1882
   d. 1817 and 1830

15. When did Peter Cooper invent *Tom Thumb*?
   a. 1828
   b. 1830
   c. 1825
   d. 1882

102

Constructed-Response Questions

Write your answers to the questions that follow in the spaces provided.

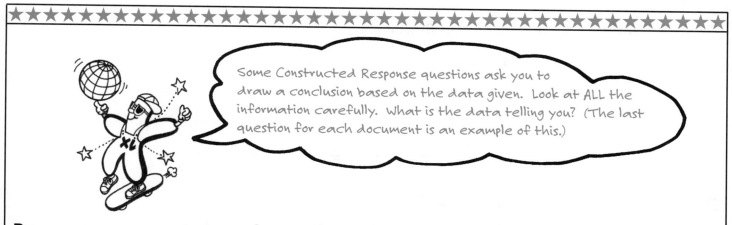

Some Constructed Response questions ask you to draw a conclusion based on the data given. Look at ALL the information carefully. What is the data telling you? (The last question for each document is an example of this.)

Base your answers to questions 1 through 4 on the poster below.

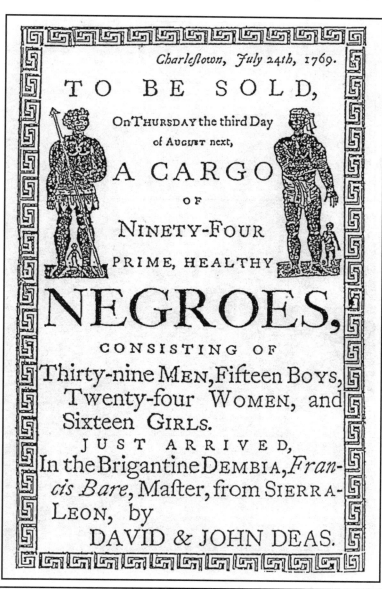

The letter ſ is really the letter S in old English!

Constructed-Response Questions

1. When and where did this poster appear?

_____

_____

_____

_____

2. What was the purpose of this poster?

_____

_____

_____

_____

_____

3. How many of the slaves were children?

_____

_____

_____

_____

4. Why do you think it was important to mention that the slaves were healthy?

_____

_____

_____

_____

_____

Constructed-Response Questions

Base your answers to questions 5 through 8 on your knowledge of social studies and the famous song below.

5. What are some goods that were transported through the Erie Canal?

_____

_____

_____

6. What moved the barges when the Erie Canal first opened?

_____

_____

_____

7. What must they do when they approach a town?

_____

_____

_____

Why?

_____

_____

_____

8. How did the invention of the steamboat affect the poet and Sal?

_____

_____

The Erie Canal

I've got a mule, her name is Sal,
Fifteen years on the Erie Canal.
She's a good old worker and a good old pal,
Fifteen years on the Erie Canal.
We've hauled some barges in our day,
Filled with lumber, coal, and hay.
And every inch of the way I know
From Albany to Buffalo.

Low Bridge, everybody down!
Low bridge, for we're comin' to a town!
You can always tell your neighbor, can always tell your pal,
If you've ever navigated on the Erie Canal.

We'd better look for a job, old gal,
Fifteen years on the Erie Canal.
You bet your life I wouldn't part with Sal,
Fifteen years on the Erie Canal.
Giddap there, Sal, we've passed that lock,
We'll make Rome 'fore six o'clock,
So one more trip and then we'll go
Right straight back to Buffalo.

Anonymous

Constructed-Response Questions

Base your answers to questions 9 through 12 on the table below.

Famous Ship Canals in the United States

Name	Location	Length	Depth (miles)	Locks (feet)	Year Opened
Beaumont–Port Arthur	United States	40	34	—	1916
Chesapeake and Delaware	United States	19	27	—	1927
Erie Canal	United States	363	7	82	1825
Houston	United States	50	40	—	1914
St. Lawrence Seaway	U.S. and Canada	2,400	17–30	—	1959

(from Time Almanac 2000 (simplified))

9. Which canal in this chart connects two countries?

_____

_____

10. Which canal is the oldest?

_____

_____

11. What do the dashes in the "Locks" column mean?

_____

_____

12. Which canal is the deepest?

_____

What do you think this canal can do that the Erie Canal cannot do?

_____

_____

IMMIGRATION TO AMERICA

After surveying the story, I can tell that:

1. Immigrants from Africa came as _____.
    a. hired helpers   b. slaves

2. People rushed to California in 1848 in search of _____.
    a gold   b. silver

3. The "New Immigrants" came from Southern European countries
_____.

    a. for religious freedom   b. to escape poverty

After looking at the objective questions and constructed-response questions, I can tell that:

4. Eli Whitney invented the _____.
    a. sewing machine   b. cotton gin

5. President Franklin D. Roosevelt reminded us that all our ancestors
were _____.
    a. farmers   b. immigrants

ANSWER BOX

1. Immigrants from Africa came as slaves.
2. People rushed to California in 1848 in search of gold.
3. The "New Immigrants" came from Southern European countries to escape poverty.
4. Eli Whitney invented the cotton gin.
5. President Franklin D. Roosevelt reminded us that all our ancestors were immigrants.

Read the following selection carefully. Stop after each section to retell the main idea in your own words.

The Story of Immigration to America

★★★

Like most immigrant families, often the father came first and sent for his family later.

Ships brought slaves from Africa to work in the fields.

Thomas Paine was a great patriot during the Revolutionary War. He had a dream for the future of this new country. He said it would become a place "for the **persecuted** lovers of civil and **religious liberty** from every part of Europe." He was almost right. The United States also became a home for people from all over the world, not just Europe. All of them hoped for a better life. It attracted adventurers, too. Some people were bored with life at home and wanted to try something new.

The first immigrants to the United States were mostly from countries like England, Scotland, and Ireland. One-fifth were slaves from Africa. After the Revolution, this brand-new country needed people. Congress passed a law in 1790. It welcomed any free white person to enter the United States and become a **citizen**.

Growth of the South

The cotton industry boomed in the South. Cotton plantations spread across the southern states. **Eli Whitney** invented the cotton gin in 1793. It would separate cotton much faster than could be done by hand. Cotton plantation owners needed workers to plant fields of cotton. So ships brought slaves from Africa. They provided free labor. No one really knows exactly how many slaves came. Although they came against their will, the slaves were immigrants. However, they could not be citizens.

The Growth of Cities

The new inventions of the Industrial Revolution caused cities to grow. Sewing machines and power tools made it easier and faster to make goods. Factories sprang up in cities across the country. New York City, an important manufacturing center, grew to four times its size from 1800 to 1850. This brought a demand for people who would work cheaply. The American government made it possible for thousands of immigrants to come.

The Gold Rush

News of the discovery of gold fields in the West spread around the world. The **California Gold Rush** started in 1848, when gold was discovered there. In two years, about 40,000 **prospectors** from the United States and Europe arrived. Thousands of Chinese men landed in California to join the Gold Rush. But only a few prospectors found gold. Others started communities and settled the West.

Cheap labor was needed to expand the country. Soon the Gold Rush was over. Chinese immigrants joined Irish and Norwegian immigrants as workers. They put down miles of railroad tracks. Trains crossed the country with record speed.

Prospectors pan for gold in a stream during the California Gold Rush in 1848.

Bad Times in Northern Europe

There were very bad times in Europe in the 1840s. The **potato famine** in Ireland killed more than a million Irish people. At least a million people left Ireland for the United States.

Populations grew in other countries in Europe. Soon, there were not enough jobs for everyone. The steam engine made the trip to America faster and cheaper. Millions of immigrants came to America from Northern Europe.

To attract immigrants to Wisconsin, the government used photographs like this to show the ample food supply.

Most immigrants looking for land to farm arrived in New York. They followed the Hudson River to the Erie Canal and then to the routes that would take them to the Midwest– Michigan, Missouri, Wisconsin, Minnesota, and the Dakotas. At this time, the offer of free land brought farmers who **emigrated** from Scandinavia and Germany. They could have as much land as they could harvest.

In 1840, Cyrus McCormick invented the **reaper**. This machine cut wheat very fast. Farmers could raise more than enough crops for their families. They produced crops to feed the rest of America, too. The country prospered, or grew rich.

Poverty in Southern Europe Brings the "New Immigrants"

The "**New Immigrants**" was the name given to those who came to the United States between 1890 and 1915. They came from Italy, Poland, Russia, Greece, and other countries in Southern Europe. Most of them were very poor. Coming to America allowed them to escape starvation.

From 1892 to 1954, more than 12 million immigrants arrived in New York harbor. Many had had a rough trip across the ocean. They were so happy to see the **Statue of Liberty** in New York harbor. France had given **Lady Liberty** to the United States. This symbol of freedom welcomed the new Americans.

Before the immigrants could go ashore in New York, they had to be checked on **Ellis Island**. This island was close to the Statue of Liberty. The government had to record the names of people coming into the country.

The Statue of Liberty, in New York harbor, welcomed the immigrants.

Inspectors checked to see that each person was in good health and was not a criminal. Those traveling first class were tested aboard ship. But the poor, traveling in steerage, waited on long lines to be processed. All newcomers were nervous about the inspection. However, only 2 percent were sent back on the same boat that had brought them.

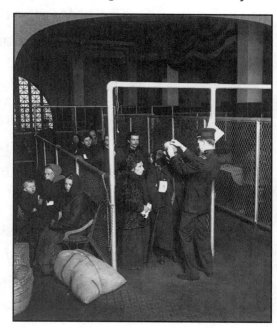

Immigrants entered a large inspection hall and were examined by doctors from the United States Health Service.

111

The New Immigrants Come to the Cities

The "New Immigrants" stayed in large cities. The days of free land had passed. This wave of immigrants did not have money to buy land. They also liked to live near other people from their **native countries**.

Worker in a Chicago meat-packing plant, 1919

In this way, they kept some of their old customs. They lived near people who spoke their language. They enjoyed the same foods.

Some had to learn completely new jobs. Others used the skills they already had. Italians became masons and worked on the New York City subways. Greeks worked in construction and in lumber camps. Jewish immigrants found work in the **garment** district of New York City. Many Polish people headed for Pittsburgh, Pennsylvania. They worked in steel mills or in mines. Others found work in the meat-packing factories of Chicago.

The different **ethnic groups** got to enjoy each other's customs. This **diversity** made America a mixture called the "**Melting Pot**."

Urban Life Was Difficult

Immigrants were not the only ones moving to the cities. New machinery put farm workers out of jobs. Their only hope was to move from a **rural area** to a city.

Urban life was very hard for the poor. More and more factories were built. The people worked in crowded, dark places with poor air. Their salaries were very low. Instead of going to school, five-year-old children went to work. Grown-ups and children worked long hours.

Many immigrants lived in overcrowded tenement houses.

Living conditions were terrible. Too many people lived in one apartment. Sometimes there was only cold water. Most places had only the heat from the stove. Without basic needs, many people became ill. Diseases spread through the buildings. These buildings were known as **tenement houses**.

Better days were coming. Workers joined together to get better conditions. Laws were passed to put a stop to **child labor**. The immigrants' courage and willingness to work changed things. They helped to build a great country.

RECITE

Give at least four reasons why immigrants flocked to America in the 1800s.

TERMS TO REMEMBER The following Names, Dates, Places, and Words about Immigration to America are important to remember. Study them carefully. The sentences will help you understand their meanings.

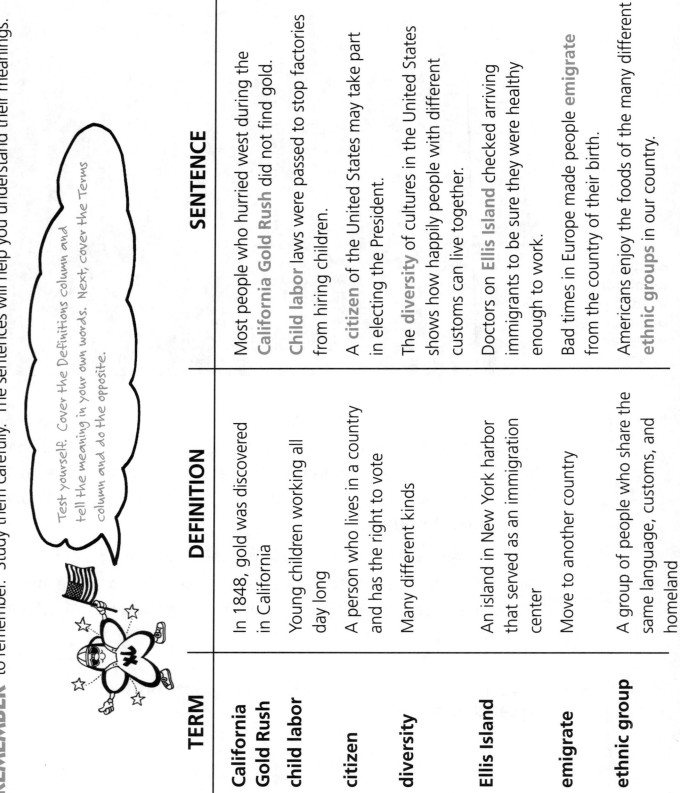

Test yourself. Cover the Definitions column and tell the meaning in your own words. Next, cover the Terms column and do the opposite.

TERM	DEFINITION	SENTENCE
California Gold Rush	In 1848, gold was discovered in California	Most people who hurried west during the **California Gold Rush** did not find gold.
child labor	Young children working all day long	**Child labor** laws were passed to stop factories from hiring children.
citizen	A person who lives in a country and has the right to vote	A **citizen** of the United States may take part in electing the President.
diversity	Many different kinds	The **diversity** of cultures in the United States shows how happily people with different customs can live together.
Ellis Island	An island in New York harbor that served as an immigration center	Doctors on **Ellis Island** checked arriving immigrants to be sure they were healthy enough to work.
emigrate	Move to another country	Bad times in Europe made people **emigrate** from the country of their birth.
ethnic group	A group of people who share the same language, customs, and homeland	Americans enjoy the foods of the many different **ethnic groups** in our country.

TERM	DEFINITION	SENTENCE
garment district	A section in New York where clothing is made	Many Jewish immigrants were tailors and worked in the **garment district**.
immigration	coming to a new country to live	Irish **immigration** increased in the 1840s because people were starving in Ireland.
industry	a type of manufacturing or business	The railroad **industry** grew after Peter Cooper invented the locomotive.
Melting Pot	A place where different ethnic groups join to make one society	The United States is the "**Melting Pot**" because all of its ethnic groups choose to become Americans, under the laws of this democracy.
native country	The country where a person is born	Some immigrants left their **native countries** to seek adventure in America.
"New Immigrants"	Immigrants who came to the United States from eastern Europe between 1890 and 1915	A huge wave of "**new immigrants**" came from countries like Russia and Greece.
persecuted	To be treated badly because of race or religion	Some of the immigrants to America had been **persecuted** and denied political freedom in their native lands.
potato famine	A food shortage in Ireland	In the 1840s, more than a million Irish people died during the **potato famine** when a disease killed their only important crop.
prospectors	People who explore an area for gold	**Prospectors** searched for gold in the mountains of California.
reaper	A machine for harvesting grain	Cyrus McCormick invented the **reaper**, helping the farmer to gather wheat faster.

115

TERM	DEFINITION	SENTENCE
religious liberty	the right to practice your own religion	The Bill of Rights in our Constitution guarantees that every American has **religious liberty**
rural	The countryside including farms and small towns	Before the Industrial Revolution, most Americans lived and farmed in **rural** areas.
Statue of Liberty – "Lady Liberty"	A symbol of freedom that stands on an island in New York harbor	**"Lady Liberty,"** the tall statue of a woman holding a torch, was a gift of friendship from France.
tenement houses	Crowded, dirty apartment buildings	Whole families lived in **tenement** houses, in small, dark, dirty rooms
urban	cities	As factories were built, people moved to **urban** areas like New York City.
Eli Whitney	Inventor of the cotton gin	**Eli Whitney's** cotton gin separated cotton fiber from the seed very quickly.

Objective Questions

Circle the correct answer choice for each question.

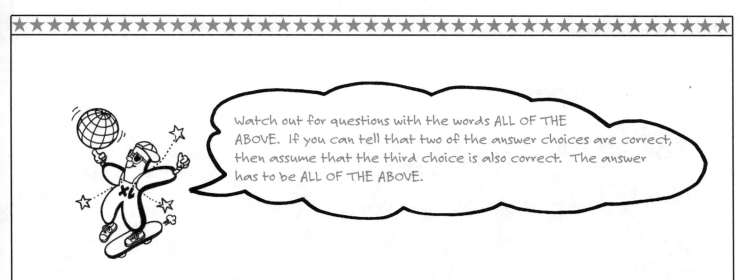

Watch out for questions with the words ALL OF THE ABOVE. If you can tell that two of the answer choices are correct, then assume that the third choice is also correct. The answer has to be ALL OF THE ABOVE.

1. Eli Whitney invented the cotton gin. This eventually led to:

   a. the tenements
   b. the California Gold Rush
   c. more slavery in the South
   d. the building of the Erie Canal

2. Ellis Island can best be described as:

   a. a first stop for many immigrants
   b. a home for many immigrants
   c. a symbol of peace
   d. a place where criminals were housed

3. Because of the Gold Rush,:

   a. many farmers got free land in the Midwest.
   b. many Chinese people came to California.
   c. more slaves were needed.
   d. children were forced to work long hours.

Base your answer to questions 4 through 6 on the map below.

NORTHWEST

MIDWEST

NORTHEAST

Washington

Montana

Oregon

Idaho

Wyoming

Nevada

Utah

Colorado

California

North Dakota

Minnesota

South Dakota

Wisconsin

Michigan

Nebraska

Iowa

Indiana

Illinois

Ohio

Kansas

Missouri

New Hampshire

Vermont

Maine

Massachusetts

New York

Rhode Island

Connecticut

Pennsylvania

New Jersey

Delaware

Maryland

Washington, D.C.

West Virginia

Virginia

Kentucky

North Carolina

Arizona

New Mexico

Oklahoma

Arkansas

Tennessee

South Carolina

Mississippi

Georgia

Alabama

Texas

Louisiana

Florida

SOUTHWEST

SOUTHEAST

Hawaii

Alaska

	Northwest
	Southwest
	Midwest
	Southeast
	Northeast

Regions of the United States

Objective Questions

4. The Midwest includes the states of:
   a. Michigan, Wisconsin, and Minnesota
   b. New York, Illinois, and the Dakotas
   c. Mississippi, Texas, and Louisiana
   d. California, Minnesota, and Wisconsin

5. According to the map:
   a. Colorado and Wyoming share a border
   b. the smallest states are in New England
   c. Idaho is in the Midwest
   d. Florida is an island

6. To go from Texas to Oregon, you travel:
   a. northeast   b. southeast
   c. northwest   d. southwest

---

7. In the cities, most immigrant groups tended to:
   a. become wealthy   b. have luxuries
   c. return to Europe   d. stay with others from their own country

8. Which of these is a person who LEFT his country?
   a. a journeyman   b. a wanderer
   c. an emigrant   d. a citizen

9. Immigrants came to America for:
   a. jobs   b. adventure
   c. a better climate   d. all of the above

10. Which area probably has the largest population?
   a. an urban area   b. a suburban area
   c. a rural area   d. a mountain area

11. Many ethnic groups together at a picnic shows:
   a. customs   b. diversity
   c. lack of cooperation d. interest in food

Objective Questions

Throughout its history, Americans have had differing views on immigration. Below are some quotes that show this. Base your answer to numbers 12 to 15 on these statements:

A. "Remember always, that all of us… are descended from immigrants and revolutionaries." Franklin D. Roosevelt

B. "Everywhere immigrants have enriched and strengthened the fabric of American life." John F. Kennedy

C. "Today a wide-open door is an invitation to national disaster." FAIR

D. "In times of shrinking expectations,… everyone feels like a victim and pushes away outsiders to defend his own corner." Oscar Handlin

E. "Give me your tired, your poor, your huddled masses yearning to breathe free, the wretched refuse of your teeming shore, send these, the homeless, tempest-tossed, to me: I lift my lamp beside the golden door." Emma Lazarus

12. Roosevelt, Kennedy, and Lazarus all:
    a. supported immigration   b. were against immigration
    c. had different views on immigration   d. didn't care about immigration

13. The two statements against immigration were made by:.
    a. Roosevelt and FAIR   b. Handlin and FAIR
    c. Handlin and Kennedy   d. Kennedy and Lazarus

14. Who does Lazarus invite into our country?
    a. those who are poor
    b. those who want freedom
    c. those who have been badly treated
    d. all of the above

15. What does FAIR think will happen if we continue to let immigrants into the country?
    a. Our nation will grow richer.
    b. People will welcome them.
    c. Disaster will strike the immigrants.
    d. There will be great trouble in the country.

120

Constructed-Response Questions

Write your answers to the questions that follow in the spaces provided.

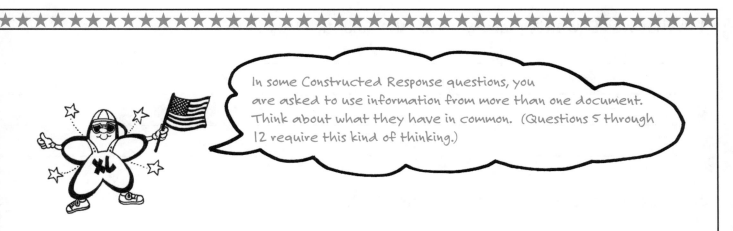

In some Constructed Response questions, you are asked to use information from more than one document. Think about what they have in common. (Questions 5 through 12 require this kind of thinking.)

Base your answers to questions 1 through 4 on the narrative below.

Edward Corsi, who later became United States Commissioner of Immigration, was a ten-year-old Italian immigrant when he sailed into New York harbor in 1907: He wrote:

> "My first impressions of the New World will always remain etched in my memory, particularly that hazy October morning when I first saw Ellis Island. The steamer Florida, fourteen days out of Naples, filled to capacity with 1600 natives of Italy, had weathered one of the worst storms in our captain's memory; and glad we were, both children and grown-ups, to leave the open sea and come at last through the Narrows into the Bay.
>
> "My mother, my stepfather, my brother Giuseppe, and my two sisters, Liberta and Helvetia, all of us together, happy that we had come through the storm safely, clustered on the foredeck for fear of separation and looked with wonder on this miraculous land of our dreams.
>
> "Giuseppe and I held tightly to Stepfather's hands, while Liberta and Helvetia clung to Mother. Passengers all about us were crowding against the rail. Jabbered conversation, sharp cries, laughs and cheers—a steadily rising din filled the air. Mothers and fathers lifted up babies so that they too could see, off to the left, the Statue of Liberty."

Constructed-Response Questions

1. What was Edward's journey across the Atlantic Ocean like?

   _____

   _____

   _____

   _____

2. What was the author's reaction when he first saw the U.S.?

   _____

   _____

   _____

   _____

3. Why?

   _____

   _____

   _____

   _____

4. How does Edward Corsi's life show that immigrants could be successful in America?

   _____

   _____

   _____

   _____

   _____

   _____

Constructed-Response Questions

Life was difficult for the children of immigrants. Examine the pictures below. Then answer the questions that follow.

Spinner in a cotton mill

A five-year-old newsie

5. Describe the lives of these immigrant children?

_____

_____

_____

_____

_____

_____

Breaker Boys of the coal mines

6. What types of work did they do?

_____

_____

7. Why do you think they worked instead of going to school?

_____

_____

_____

Constructed-Response Questions

Base your answers to questions 8 through 12 on the pie graph below.

Alien Immigration to the U.S. by Chief Ports: 1904

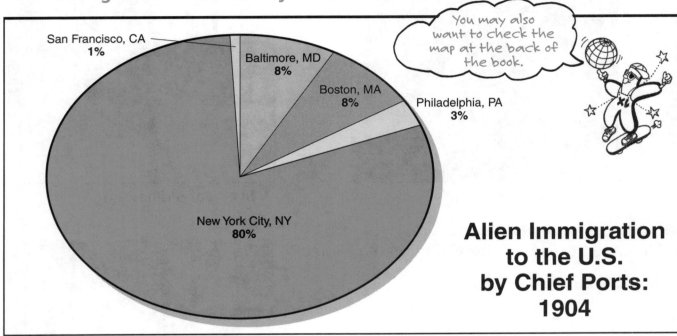

8. Through which port did most Americans enter the U.S.?

_____

9. How many ports were located on the West Coast of the U.S.?

_____

10. How many ports were on the East Coast?

_____

11. How many ports were in the Midwest? Why?

_____

_____

12. What famous sight would most immigrants would probably see first in the U.S.?

_____

DOCUMENT-BASED QUESTION

Directions: The task below is based on documents 1 through 6. It will test your ability to work with historical documents as well as your knowledge of social studies. Study each document, and answer the questions that follow. They will help you to organize your essay.

Historical Background:

The Industrial Revolution brought great change to the cities of the Northeast. Some changes were good and brought improvements to the cities and their people. Other changes brought problems.

Task:

Part A is made up of short-answer questions. After reading the essay question below, answer each question fully. Use the information in the documents and your knowledge of social studies for your answers.

Essay Question:

What was the effect of the Industrial Revolution on the cities of the Northeast? In your answer be sure to include:

- In what ways cities grew and prospered.

- How the new inventions helped business grow.

- How it affected immigrant workers and their families.

Document-Based Question

Part A—Short-Answer Questions

Directions: Study each document and answer the questions that follow. Base your answers on the documents provided as well as your knowledge of social studies.

DOCUMENT 1

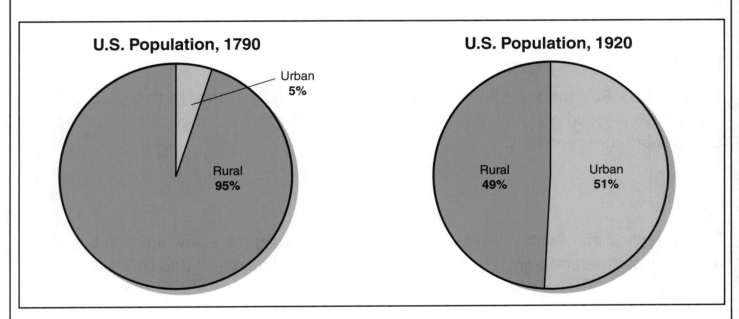

The pie graphs above show where people in the United States lived in 1790 and in 1920. Use this information to answer the questions below.

1. In 1790, where did most of the people live?

_____

_____

2. By 1920, how had that changed?

_____

_____

3. What was a main reason for this change in population?

_____

_____

126

Document-Based Question

★★

DOCUMENT 2

The Boston area became the first region of the nation to experience industrialization. Plants such as this textile factory were built. Soon the amount of American exports (goods sold to other countries) was greater than the amount of imports (goods bought from other countries).

Early Industrial Plant in Boston

1. How did inventions in transportation, such as the steamboat and railroad, help factories like this grow and prosper?

_____

_____

2. How did factories affect the population of the cities?

_____

_____

3. Why is it good when a country exports more goods than it imports?

_____

127

★★

Document-Based Question

DOCUMENT 3

New York City became a center of fashion. The garment district provided new styles of clothing, which a growing number of people could now afford.

Life in New York: The Breath of Fashion—5th Avenue

1. The people in this picture have a good life. How can you tell?

_____

_____

_____

2. How did inventions like the cotton gin, the sewing machine, and the light bulb help New York City's garment district grow?

_____

_____

_____

★★

DOCUMENT 4

Leonard Covello has described his family's first American home and his mother's reaction to running water in the hallway. (Many immigrants had grown up in the old country, carrying water from a well):

> "Our first home in America was a tenement flat near the East River at 112th Street....The sunlight and fresh air of our mountain home in [southern Italy] were replaced by four walls and people over and under and on all sides of us, until it seemed that humanity from all corners of the world had [come together] in this section of New York City....
>
> "The cobbled streets. The endless...rows of tenement buildings that shut out the sky. ...The clanging of bells and the screeching of sirens as a fire broke out somewhere in the neighborhood. Dank (damp) hallways. Long flights of wooden stairs and the toilet in the hall. And the water, which to my mother was one of the great wonders of America — water with just the twist of a handle, and only a few (steps) from the kitchen. It took her a long time to get used to this luxury....
>
> "It was Mrs. Accurso who put her arm comfortingly about my mother's shoulder and led her... into the hall and showed her the water faucet. 'Courage! You will get used to it here. See! Isn't it wonderful how the water comes out?'
>
> Through her tears my mother managed a smile."

★★

★★

1. Mrs. Covello had mixed feelings about her new home. Describe what she liked and why.

_____

_____

_____

_____

_____

_____

_____

_____

_____

2. What did she find unpleasant? Why?

_____

_____

_____

_____

_____

In many buildings, tenants got their water from a community faucet in the hallway on each floor.

3. In what ways was her old home probably different?

_____

_____

_____

_____

_____

★★

Document-Based Question

DOCUMENT 5

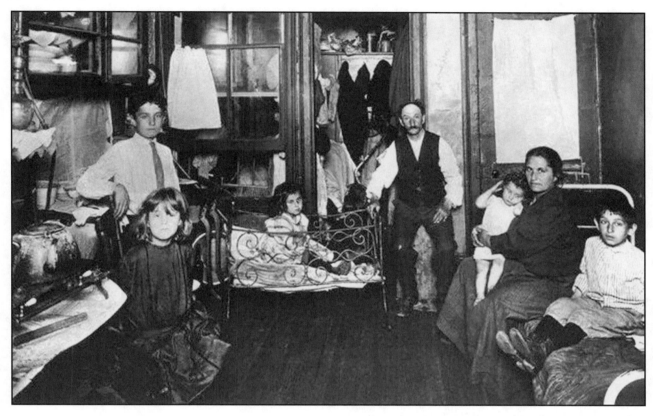

An immigrant family's tenement apartment in NYC, 1910. The family shown used this room for cooking, eating, and as a bedroom for their children. The parents had the tiny bedroom seen in the back.

1. What makes cooking, eating, relaxing, and sleeping difficult for this family?

_____

_____

_____

2. What do you suppose life was like for the children?

_____

_____

_____

Document-Based Question

Some workers in a textile (cloth) factory

One harmful effect of the Industrial Revolution is pictured above. Tell what you know about it.

_____

_____

_____

_____

_____

_____

_____

_____

Document-Based Question

Part B—Essay

Directions: Review the documents in Part A and your answers. They will help you to write the essay below.

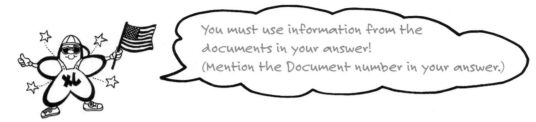

You must use information from the documents in your answer!
(Mention the Document number in your answer.)

Historical Background:

The Industrial Revolution brought great change to the cities of the Northeast. Some changes were good and brought improvements to the cities and their people. Other changes brought problems.

Task:

Use the documents in Part A, your answers, and your knowledge of social studies to write the essay below.

Essay Question:

What was the effect of the Industrial Revolution on the cities of the Northeast? In your answer be sure to include:

• In what ways cities grew and prospered.

• How the new inventions helped business grow.

• How it affected immigrant workers and their families.

Use the graphic organizer on the next page to organize your answer!

133

GRAPHIC ORGANIZER

Take notes. Do not use full sentences.

Doc.	Notes	Doc.	Notes	Doc.	Notes

Document-Based Question

_____

_____

_____

_____

_____

_____

_____

_____

_____

_____

_____

_____

_____

_____

_____

_____

_____

_____

_____

Document-Based Question

Go to the Editor's Page ➡

EDITOR'S PAGE ★★★★★★★★★★★★★★★★★★★★★★★★★★★★★★★★★★★★

Use the checklist below to be sure that
you wrote a clear and detailed essay on
the topic.

Did you...

☐ **use the information in the Historical Background to start the Introduction?**
(Did you state the information in your own words?)

☐ **include a transitional sentence to explain what your essay is about?**
(example: In this essay I will show/demonstrate/prove/state...)

☐ **answer each part of the essay question in a separate paragraph?**

☐ **remember to answer ALL parts of the essay question?**

☐ **add details to support your ideas?**

☐ **mention the document numbers you used to back up your answers?**

☐ **write a conclusion that sums up your ideas?**
(examples: Thus,/Therefore,/In conclusion, Briefly,...)

Check your writing for errors.
Did you...

☐ **capitalize all names of people
and places as well as the first word
of each sentence?**

☐ **limit your sentence to one "and" so you don't run the risk of
run-on sentences?**
(This isn't fool proof, but it helps many kids.)

☐ **check the spelling of all words you used that are right there in the
question or document?**

☐ **remember to use correct punctuation (.?!) at the end of each sentence?**

★★★

Map of the United States ★★★★★★★★★★★★★★★★

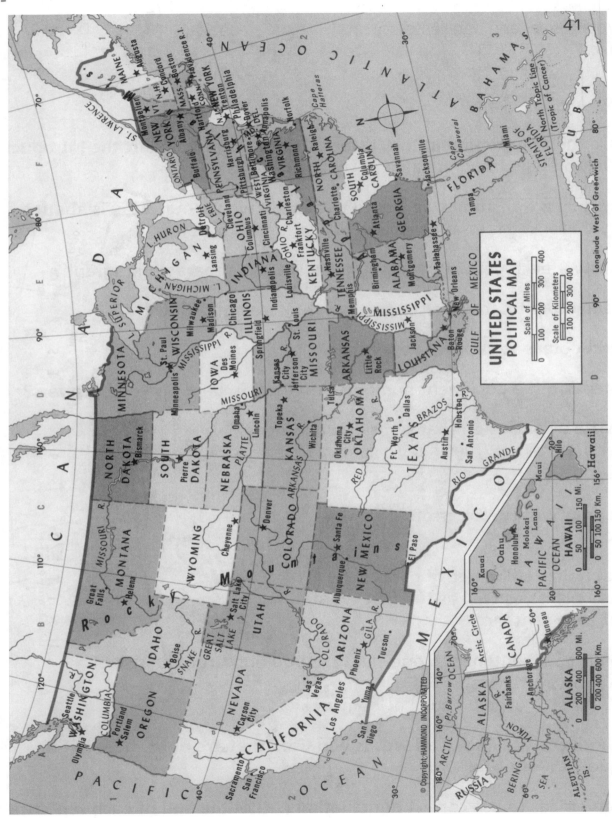